eBay Business Strategies Anyone Can Learn

A Step By Step Guide To Starting, Marketing and Profiting From Your Own eBay Business

By: TAK Technology LLC

EBAY BUSINESS STRATEGIES ANYONE CAN LEARN

TAK Technology, LLC
179 South Main Street
Gardner, MA 01440 U.S.A

ISBN - 978-0-9826947-2-5

Note: This book contains the opinions and ideas of its author. It is intended to provide helpful and informative material on the subject matter covered. It is sold with the understanding that the author and publisher are not engaged in rendering professional services in the book. If the reader requires personal assistance or advice, a competent professional should be consulted.

The author and publisher specifically disclaim any responsibility for any liability, loss, or risk, personal or otherwise, which is incurred as a consequence, directly or indirectly, of the use and application of any of the contents of this book.

Introduction

Hello! I would like to thank you for your purchase of "eBay Business Strategies Anyone Can Learn". Every technique that is shared with you my husband and I use or used in our business. I remember sitting right where you are now. You want to start a profitable online business and have no idea where to begin. We began where most do, on eBay. We have put together a book of basic steps to take in beginning a profitable eBay business.

Keep in mind that eBay should only be a stepping stone on your path to online business success. With the constant change in eBay policies and rising fees it may be difficult to find lasting success on eBay but it is still a great place to begin because of the exposure you get to consumers. That is why we have included the basic steps you need. If you want a more advanced eBay education we suggest eBay for Dummies the All in One Desk Reference.

The techniques we are going to share with you are ones we have used or use daily in our own business so if you are having trouble, have questions, or are interested in learning more about a particular marketing technique.

Please contact us at - takteam@ourgrnbusiness.com.

Happy Reading!

Kristin and Tom

P.S. We would suggest you go through this book section by section slowly. There is a lot of information and it could get overwhelming if you try to jump in all at once. Each section is broken up into smaller sub sections so that you do not get overwhelmed.

<u>Disclaimer</u>

This book is designed to provide information on starting, launching, marketing, and building an online business. It is sold with the understanding that the publisher and author are not engaged in rendering legal, accounting or other professional services. If legal or other expert assistance is required, the services of a competent professional should be sought.

eBay Business Strategies Anyone Can Learn is not a get rich quick scheme. Anyone who decides to start a business must expect to invest a lot of time and effort into it. For many people an online business is more lucrative than working a 8-5 job but you have to have the drive and motivation to build a solid, growing, rewarding businesses.

Every effort has been made to make this book as complete and accurate as possible. However, there may be mistakes, both typographical and in content. This book should be used only as a general guide and not as the ultimate source of Internet Marketing information. This book contains information on Internet Marketing and online business building that is current only up to the printing date.

The purpose of this book is to educate, the author and publisher shall have neither liability nor responsibility to any person or entity with respect to any loss or damage caused, or alleged to have been caused, directly or indirectly, by the information contained in this book.

Table of Contents

Chapter Two Create Listings that Raise your Profits

Chapter Five Expand Your Business

Chapter One

Target a Market

1. Start Using eBay Correctly from the Beginning

A. Find what you need on eBay's homepage

Most eBay sellers begin selling like it is an online tag sale, they find a few items to sell, set up their auctions, then sit back and hope they'll sell their items at a profit instead of a loss. That's not how you are going to do it. In this book, you'll learn how to build a solid foundation for an exciting eBay business that will bring in strong, consistent profits. We'll show you how to use powerful market research tools available to find a hot market you can sell to. Armed with this information, you'll be able to plan and build an eBay business based on your skills and start selling right away. Even if you're interested in becoming a hobby seller, that's fine. Auctioning off a few items you've got around the house is a great way to start your own eBay selling career.

All the examples and strategies in this course refer to eBay.com; it is eBay's US-based site and their main site. If you live outside the US and are planning to target buyers specifically in your home country, you'll want to check out eBay's international site for your country -

- Germany: eBay.de
- United Kingdom: eBay.co.uk
- Australia: eBay.com.au
- Canada: eBay.ca

eBay's full list of international sites is listed at the footer of the main page. No matter where you live, when you're getting started it's best to stick with eBay.com. While I am sure you have been to eBay.com before, let's take a look around the eBay so you start to get comfortable with it from a selling perspective. As you explore eBay's homepage ask yourself questions like -

- How will my future customers use this site element?
- Could I use this feature to attract new customers?
- How do I make my products and services appear here?
- What kinds of listings or ads would work best here?

a. Header and navigation

eBay's header and navigation appear at the top right of most pages on eBay's site, giving you a quick way to jump to the basic sections that make up the site. The Buy tab allows you to search for products by category and subcategory rather than by a keyword search. The Sell tab will be one of your most visited links as an eBay business owner because this is where you begin the process of listing an item for sell on eBay. The My eBay tab lets you see an overview of all your eBay transactions and communications. The Community tab offers news and resources that connect you with other eBay members. The Help tab contains a wide variety of helpful learning tools like eBay policies, eBay feature definitions, policies, and tutorials.

b. Search box

Most eBay visitors go straight to this search box to type in their search terms. Any active listings that contain those keywords will then be displayed. Keep this important point in mind because when you're an eBay seller, keyword searches will be an all-important consideration when creating your listing titles.

c. Specialty sites

The "quick links" box at the top of the left column points to a few of eBay's more specialized sites -

- eBay Motors: The dedicated site for buying and selling vehicles
- eBay Stores: Sellers can create their own mini-sites or "stores" within eBay to sell different products
- Deals: Daily deals from trusted sellers

d. Categories

Everything sold on eBay has at least one category, so shopper's breakdown their search to find listings that interest them. You can link to the category you're looking for from the drop-down menu under the search box, or the list in the left-hand column. There are also a series of links to other eBay companies that you'll want to learn more about like PayPal, Skype, and Kijiji. The main page displays announcements, special offers, and other features. eBay often changes the layout of this section. You'll see "Featured Items" here, as well as "NEW from eBay.com" section with links to new services and promotions. It would be a good idea to o click around and learn more about what's behind all these links.

As a visitor to eBay, you're free to browse many sections of the site, reviewing listings, and learning more about how eBay works. Before you can do any bidding, buying, or selling, you'll need to register and create your eBay User ID. To register, go to (https://signin.ebay.com/ws/eBayISAPI.dll?SignIn) You'll be taken to a secure page, click register and you will be prompted to -

- Enter your personal information
- Create a User ID and password
- Agree to eBay's terms of use

Choosing a user ID is easier if you have some idea what you're planning to sell. When you're just starting out, this can feel like a difficult choice. How can you know what you plan to sell until you've done the research? If you fall into this category, choose an ID that reflects one of your top areas of interest or expertise. Keep it general, and if you have to choose another ID once your business takes off, you can: eBay allows you to change your user ID once every 30 days.

Your User ID can't be an email address or web address. For more details you should look at eBay's guidelines. In the Terms of Use section, review eBay's User Agreement and Privacy Policy and click the checkbox to acknowledge that you agree to abide by their terms of service. eBay will send an email with the subject line "eBay Registration" to the email address you entered. To complete your registration, you'll need to find this email and follow the instructions in it to prove that you are the owner of that email address. Now you're set up to buy and sell on eBay.

The eBay Toolbar is free software you can download and add to your web browser. It 's a great tool that lets you instantly access many of eBay's features, even when you 're off eBay's site and browsing the rest of the Web. It gives you access to features like -

- Search eBay.
- Quick access to key eBay areas
- Alerts
- Buying and selling status
- eBay Favorites

If you're serious about selling on eBay, you should install this toolbar. However the eBay Toolbar is only available for Microsoft's Internet Explorer browser. To download -

- Visit the eBay Toolbar page and click the big orange Download now button.
- In the window that appears, click Save file to save the file to your computer.
- Find the file and double-click to open it.

Follow the instructions, when you finish, your browser should open with the toolbar displayed. To use all the toolbar's features, you'll need to sign in and register with the User ID you created. Once you've done that, take a few minutes to explore the toolbar's quick links and buttons. You can also click the Customize button to view more available buttons and adjust your settings for signing in, viewing security alerts, and so on.

B. Set up the key pages on eBay

You're ready to start exploring the rest of eBay.com. You'll find that the site is huge, even experienced eBayers like us have trouble finding key pages when we need them. We encourage you to bookmark any eBay site pages you find useful. As you continue to use eBay and discover new sections and resources, get in the habit of adding new pages to this folder as you discover them, it will make your eBay experience smooth right from the start. Click Favorites or Bookmarks on your browser, then create a new folder and name it "eBay." As you're exploring, you can add any page you're viewing to this folder. Then it's there when you want to return to it later. To start add these pages -

- Learning Center (http://pages.ebay.com/education/index.html)
- "New to eBay" pages (http://pages.ebay.com/help/newtoebay/index.html)
- eBay Site Map (http://pages.ebay.com/sitemap.html)
- A to Z index (http://pages.ebay.com/help/index/A.html)
- My eBay (http://my.ebay.com/)
- Seller Central (http://pages.ebay.com/sellercentral)
- Advanced Search (http://search.ebay.com/ws/search/AdvSearch)
- eBay My World (http://myworld.ebay.com/)
- eBay Keywords (http://buy.ebay.com/)
- eBay Pulse (http://pulse.ebay.com/)

C. Create a PayPal account

PayPal is an online payment method that is used in most online transactions worldwide. It's not necessary to have a PayPal account to sell on eBay but we recommend it. As well as being eBay's preferred payment method, PayPal is secure. It encrypts sensitive information and allows you to transfer money or accept credit/debit cards at low cost. It's fast, easy, and free to set up. Follow these instructions -

- Visit PayPal.com and click Sign Up Today at the bottom of the page.
- Select your country and language, then choose what kind of account you're opening: Personal, Premier, or Business. Click the Start Now button underneath the account type you want.

  Personal account - This type of account is not recommended for selling, but it's good for buyers. It's free for you to accept PayPal payments with this account, but you're quite restricted -- you can accept credit or debit payments, but you only get 5 per year and they cost 4.9% + $0.30 USD per transaction

  Premier account - We recommend you choose a Premier account because it allows you to accept all forms of payment (including credit cards) for a small percentage of the amount received -- 1.9% to 2.9%, plus a flat fee of $0.30 USD per transaction.

  Business account - If you have an established business with a bank account in the business name, choose the Business account option. As with the premier account, you can receive all payment types for a flat fee of $0.30 USD per transaction, plus 1.9% to 2.9% of sale cost. Your business name will show up in your clients' statements, and you can allow multiple users to access the account. You also get e-commerce tools that are useful as your business grows, including financial reporting and payment automation tools.

- Enter your personal information, including name and contact information as they are listed on your bank accounts. The email address and password you provide on this form will be used to log in to your PayPal account. For added security, use different passwords for PayPal and eBay. Your password should include a combination of letters, numbers, and special characters, and it should be at least 8 characters long.
- Choose two security questions and answers.
- Enter the characters at the bottom of your screen exactly as you see them in the space provided. This is a security measure -- it's used to make sure that you're a person, and not just a piece of PayPal-sign-up software.
- Read the User Agreement and Privacy Policy, then select I Agree -- Create My Account at the bottom of the page.
- Complete your registration by opening the sign-up email confirmation sent to you by PayPal and clicking the link they provide to you. This will activate your PayPal account. Then, you'll be directed back to PayPal, where you will need to enter your password. This confirms your email address. Now you have a PayPal account.

D. Protect yourself from fraud

On eBay there are scammers sneaking around trying to steal people's money or identities. Don't worry if you're careful, it's easy to tell the good eBayers from the bad.

a. Protect your account information from theft

Scammers try to gain access to user's eBay or PayPal account information by sending fake emails claiming to be from eBay or PayPal. This process is known as "phishing." Phishing emails look like the real thing to fool some recipients into clicking through to a fake website and entering personal information such as their name, User ID, and password. The scammers can then access that person's account and use it to set up fake auctions or drain the funds from it. Another phishing strategy is to include a link that looks harmless but when clicked releases a virus designed to gather your personal information from your computer. These messages look believable, but you can spot them by looking for the signs -

- The email doesn't show up in your eBay My Messages inbox
- The email doesn't address you by name
- The URL looks unusual

If an email looks suspicious, don't click any links it contains. If it's asking you to take an action such as updating your account information, you can always open a browser window and go to eBay or PayPal, if the message is a real, you'll be able to find it after logging in. eBay and PayPal will never request your password by email. PayPal's Security Center has more information about buying securely through PayPal. eBay also offers a spoof email tutorial to educate you about what hacker emails look like and how you can protect your account.

b. Avoid scams that target buyers

- Beware of sellers with bad feedback
- If it looks too good to be true, it probably is
- Read descriptions carefully
- Look out for "shill" bidding

The best way to protect yourself as a buyer is to walk away from any auction you have a bad feeling about and assume that if it looks too good to be true, it is.

2. Become a Bidder

A. <u>Learn by buying</u>

The best way to learn how to sell on eBay is to buy on eBay. By experiencing the auction process as a buyer, you'll learn a lot about how to make buyers happy when you start selling. You can also start building a positive Feedback rating and your credibility as an eBayer by buying small items on eBay. To start learning the ropes, pick an item you'd like to purchase and see if you're able to find that item for sale on eBay. While looking around, focus on the techniques that various sellers use to get you to check out their listings. While you're shopping, ask these questions -

- What do you find appealing about certain auctions?
- What draws your eye to a listing?
- What elements of an auction persuade you to make a bid?
- What information are sellers not including that you want to know as a buyer?

Once you've spent some time browsing around eBay and found some items that you wouldn't mind purchasing, it's time to make a few bids. When you find an auction you want to bid on, click the blue Place Bid button located below the current bid amount at the top of every auction. This will take you to the Place a Bid page. You can enter your maximum bid in the space provided and then confirm that it's correct. eBay will send you an email informing you that your bid has been registered. Most of the bidding takes place in the final few minutes of an auction, so it's a good idea to wait until the last 5 minutes to place your bid so you don't drive the price up. If someone outbids you, you'll receive an email letting you know and you can place another bid. This goes on until the auction ends.

After winning your first auction, pay attention to how the checkout process works, and how the seller completes the transaction. When you receive your item, you should leave Feedback for the seller. As well as leaving sellers an overall positive, neutral, or negative rating, buyers can also leave Detailed Seller Ratings which are anonymous. DSRs will be important for you when you start selling because they help determine how high your items get listed in the search results.

DSRs are average ratings for four areas - item as described, communication, shipping time, and shipping and handling charges. When rating your sellers DSRs ask yourself these questions -

- Did the item meet your expectations and was it as described in the auction listing?

- Did the seller email you after the auction, or did you have to contact them? What was their general communication with you like?
- How long did it take for your item to arrive?
- Were the shipping and handling charges fair? How long did it take for your item to arrive?

If you were pleased with the buying process you experienced with a seller then you should write down what they did and try to do it yourself when you start running your own auctions. Maintaining good DSRs is crucial for the success of your business on eBay. Your own buyers will appreciate it as much as you did and they'll be more likely to leave you positive Feedback or buy from you again. Your experience as a buyer should also teach you the basics of how to put together a professional-looking auction listing. When you're surfing around eBay look at the different auction strategies like -

- Buy It Now pricing
- Low starting bids
- Highlighting listings on the search results page
- Using different numbers or styles of images

The techniques that make you want to bid are likely to work well on other buyers too, make sure to include them in your own auction listings when you start selling.

B. Start building good Feedback

You may have noticed while browsing around the site that all eBay users have a "Feedback" page where other users can leave positive, neutral, or negative Feedback about each transaction. eBay's Feedback system is one of its core features. Your Feedback profile represents your eBay credibility, and when you start selling it gives buyers confidence that you can be trusted. Starting as a buyer is one of the best ways to quickly establish credibility on eBay. Make your payments on time and be friendly and courteous to the seller.

Once you've safely received your item, leave Feedback and Detailed Seller Ratings for the seller. When the transaction is completed, ask for Feedback. Reciprocal Feedback is an accepted practice on eBay. A seller cannot leave a buyer negative Feedback, so many don't leave any at all. But if you request it, and leave the seller a glowing recommendation, they'll usually return the favor. It doesn't matter what you buy, as long as you buy enough items to start building some impressive Feedback. There are many inexpensive deals with low shipping costs. To leave Feedback and DSRs after you've bought an item on eBay -

- Go to your My eBay page.
- Click the "Won" link in the left-hand column
- Click the Leave Feedback button and you'll see a page containing a list of items you've bought, with space to leave Feedback.
- After you choose Positive, Neutral, or Negative Feedback you are taken to a page where you can rank sellers on their Detailed Seller Ratings.

A common buyer mistake is to not read the listings carefully and then complain about something that was clearly stated. You can avoid a lot of potentially negative situations by reading the entire description carefully and not bidding on items that are damaged or come with high shipping fees. If something goes wrong, don't automatically leave negative Feedback or dock points off one of the DSRs. Always contact the seller first and politely explain why you're not satisfied. Most sellers will try to fix the problem rather than receive negative Feedback or low DSRs.

Feedback is now so important to sellers that it's more vital you make sure the issue cannot be resolved another way. New users don't realize what a stain negative Feedback is on a seller's record. For most sellers, being threatened with negative Feedback is enough to kick-start them into handling a problem. eBay has made negative and neutral Feedback reversible, so if you do realize you've made a mistake, you'll be able to change it. If new users try to leave negative Feedback, eBay displays a warning page reminding them to try to resolve the problem by emailing the seller first.

Low DSR ratings are a huge problem for sellers. They're a relatively new feature on eBay, so many buyers don't realize that a perfect 5 means there were no problems. It's not something that a seller has to go to superhuman lengths to achieve. By leaving good DSRs you'll make sellers happy and guarantee good feedback for yourself.

3. Set up your First Auction

A. <u>Create a listing</u>

You've opened an eBay seller's account and a PayPal account. It's time to start selling. You'll need to find something to sell. It's easiest to start how most sellers do, find something lying around your house that you don't need anymore. Your test item should be small and easy to ship. It should be something that you won't mind selling for a dollar, plus shipping. Once you've found something to sell, visit the Sell Your Item page and click through to sign in to the SYI form. It will guide you through the steps of creating a listing and provide information like suggested categories for your item or average starting price.

If you need to stop working on your listing you can save your listing and complete it later. You can save listings as templates and reuse them, which will save you time as you sell more. eBay only saves one listing, so if you start a new one you'll lose this one. Listing items will get faster once you're used to it. There are plenty of other tools and strategies to streamline the process that we'll cover later. eBay gives you many choices for your listing format but to get started just choose the Online Auction format and run your auction for a week. Every decision affects sales, here's a list of what you need to include in your listing -

a. Category

You've got your item, first select its category. If you're not sure which category to choose, do a search for similar items and see what they use, or search categories for the one where you find the most similar items listed. You should do this with every listing you post. Find other sellers offering the same kinds of items you're selling and model your listing after theirs. Following the lead of successful listings can save you some time. You can search categories from the Sell page using the Browse categories link.

b. Item Specifics

On the Sell Your Item form, you may see "Item Specifics." Be sure to fill it in if it's there because it helps eBay deliver the most relevant results to potential buyers. In some categories, many of the fields will be filled automatically as soon as you type in the product name, leaving only a few fields to fill in manually. eBay is always adding new categories with these pre-filled "product details".

c. Title

Use descriptive keywords and their variations for your title. Stick to the facts and avoid adjectives. Nobody searches eBay for "cool" or "awesome". Using keywords that describe brand, color, style, size, and category will help shoppers find your item. Think of keywords you would use to find your item.

d. Photograph

A quality photograph is essential for selling your items and including one in your listing is free. Would you buy anything without knowing what it looked like? Oddss are, you wouldn't, and neither would anyone else. For some listings you'll want to add extra photos but be aware that adding features costs extra and can eat up your profits.

e. Item description

Your item description is the most critical part of your listing, describe your item in detail. The key is to put yourself in your bidders' shoes. When describing the features of your item, focus on how they'll help your bidder. The item description is the perfect place to tell the bidder about yourself, your dedication to customer service, and your professional attitude. You need to reassure your bidder you're credible, reliable, and honest.

f. Starting price

It's usually best to start the bidding in your auction at 99 cents. This will minimize your fees and attract your first bidders. You can spare yourself some time by doing some research before you set your starting price - Search for your item (and similar listings) using the "completed listings" option of the Advanced Search feature. This will let you see how many items just like yours were listed and what their final sale price was. If they didn't sell for 99 cents, you probably want to find a different item to sell.

g. Terms and conditions

In the terms and conditions, you'll need to get into the fine print about payments, shipping and handling, Feedback, warranty and refund policy. Shipping is a big part of DSRs, so make sure your shipping charges and policies are clear and fair. Include a note urging bidders to contact you if they have any questions.

h. Links containing more information

You can include links in your item description that help to promote or sell your item, but eBay has a strict links policy. They are particular about where your links go. As a general rule, you can link to almost any eBay page you want but you can't link to pages outside eBay unless the only thing on those pages is information relevant to your auction.

Once you've finished creating a listing on the Sell Your Item form, preview it, make sure everything looks okay. Then post it on eBay. The auction goes live as soon as you post it, or you can schedule a start time using the how you're selling section of the SYI form. Then sit back and start monitoring your listings and the messages you receive. Don't worry if you don't get many bids the first few days, more than half of all winning bids are placed in the last hour of the auction. You can track all of your eBay buying and selling activity by using the eBay Toolbar or checking up in My eBay.

If you see a sale notification in your email inbox, don't immediately assume it's legitimate. Scammers may send fake notification messages that look like they're from eBay but clicking a link in one could infect your computer with a virus, or even compromise the security of your financial information. Any legitimate messages from eBay will appear in the my messages section of your My eBay page, so check there before clicking any links contained in a message.

B. Complete the sale and leave Feedback

If you've written a good description and included a quality photo, and the item looks like a good deal, there's no reason it shouldn't sell. Almost 60% of all auctions on eBay end without receiving a bid, so you're already ahead if your item sells. If your item didn't sell don't get discouraged but you need to find out why. Were there spelling errors in the headline? Was it listed in the right category? Was the starting price too high?

You'll need to search through the completed listings for similar items that did and didn't sell. Once your item sells, it's up to you to complete the sale. You'll see the sale and the buyer identified on your My eBay page, and you'll get an email from eBay letting you know that another user has agreed to purchase your item. If you don't receive payment immediately, you should email the winning bidder, click the send invoice button in the notification message, to inform them of the final price, which should include shipping. Also let them know when you are expecting payment.

After receiving your money and putting the package in the mail, it's always good customer service to send an email telling the buyer that you have sent the item. Include information such as the package tracking number and estimated arrival time. Remember to thank them for their business and ask them to leave positive Feedback. Neutral or negative Feedback will warn other buyers to stay away from you and they will. If your account has a even few negative Feedback marks, you'll get fewer bidders and a lower sale price on items you sell. If you have positive ratings, buyers won't hesitate to bid early, bid often, and drive that sale price up. Here are a few tips to build good feedback -

- Ask for Positive Feedback whenever possible
- Respond to buyers quickly and ship quickly
- Ask buyers to contact you before leaving Feedback if there are any issues
- Make sure after you ship the item you leave your buyer feedback

The higher your Feedback rating, the better your reputation, and the more comfortable buyers will be bidding on your auctions. eBayers take Feedback seriously, and you should too. Your feedback affects your DSRs and your DSRs determine the position of your listings in eBay's search results.

C. Analyze your auction

After you've completed a few auctions and gained a better understanding of the buying and selling process, it's time to ask yourself, "What have I learned?" Even though you may have put a lot of thought, effort, and time into building the perfect listing, there's always room for improvement. The good news is, you can get lots of free help analyzing your transactions from eBay bidders. After you list your item, you may receive questions from potential buyers in your eBay account. Pay attention to these questions. You may begin to notice patterns of potential bidders asking the same or similar questions.

The most common questions usually relate to issues such as overseas shipping costs, the condition of the item, and the speed of shipping, you can save yourself some time and effort if you include this information in your listings. You can answer general questions in your frequently asked questions section because something's in your listing doesn't mean people will read it. Most people will ask about information that's staring them in the face.

That's why it's a good idea to take advantage of the Frequently Asked Questions feature that pops up when visitors click the Ask the Seller a Question button on your listing. Answer all the repeated questions there and you'll avoid extra emailing. Answering questions individually may not seem like a big issue now but if your listing hundreds of auctions a week. You'll quickly find that cutting the number of emails you have to write will make a difference.

a. How many visitors did your auction get?

When you're creating a listing, eBay gives you the option of including a visitor counter at the bottom of your auction. We recommend that you use it, otherwise you have no way of tracking how many people are opening your listing. Set it up so you can see it but it's not visible on your site. If only a few people visit your auction, the problem is likely in your title. The other explanation could be that your item is in the wrong category.

b. How many bids did your auction get?

It's easy to look at the bidding history of your item or anyone else's. Just click the bids link on the Completed Item page or the link beside history on your My eBay page. If you're getting lots of visitors but no bids, the problem is in your description. Try to improve the product description of your next auction by including more information.

Getting started on eBay is easy so you don't want to stay at the beginner level making beginner money. Do some homework, get comfortable browsing the site and gain some basic experience so you'll know what you're doing when you start a real eBay business. After buying and selling a few small items, you should feel much more at ease navigating and using eBay. That's when you can start thinking more seriously about your future eBay business. Running a few practice auctions will help determine what equipment you're going to need to run your business efficiently. Don't be afraid to make some mistakes. Remember every mistake is a step to learning what works.

4. What should you Sell

A. <u>Choosing your product</u>

A lot of inexperienced sellers spend hours researching what the hottest items are when trying to decide what to sell. They think the way to make money on eBay is to sell mp3 players, home electronics, and video games. The problem with this strategy is that so many other people have the same idea. If you go this route it'll be hard to generate enough profit to earn a decent full-time or even part-time income. It's not just other eBay members that you have to worry about but powersellers. Powersellers are seasoned eBay merchants who have built up a big customer base, earned a good reputation, and established long-term relationships with suppliers.

They also get discounts on the Final Value Fees they pay to eBay and because they sell so much product, they can afford to sell at lower prices. Powersellers know their product lines thoroughly, and can tell when a hot product is suddenly cooling off. Instead of trying compete with the heavyweights for the hot products, we recommend that you do some in-depth product research to find lesser-known products that will sell well, in categories that suit your interest and expertise.

It's not enough to pick something that will sell once or twice on eBay, you need something that you can really sell. Identifying what will sell and what won't is not a talent or a gift, it's the result of research. Here are three questions to figure out if the product you're considering will attract buyers -

- Is this item scarce?
- Is this item desirable?
- Is this item in demand?

If you think about it, this makes sense an item that is scarce and desirable is more likely to achieve a higher price than something that no one likes and is easy to find. If your item suddenly increased in demand, the increased buyer competition will drive up the price even more particularly during the kind of bidding frenzy that happens on eBay.

The research methods you'll learn in the next lesson will answer these questions for you so you'll have a good idea if an item will sell BEFORE you invest time and energy in it. When you're researching what items to sell on eBay, start by thinking about subjects you're interested in and finding products to sell that relate to them.

a. Following your own interests will mean profits

There are good reasons for focusing on things you're interested in -

- You'll know the market better
- You'll sell your items more effectively
- You'll build your credibility and gain a competitive advantage
- You'll build better relationships with customers
- You'll be able to spot trends better

Don't limit yourself to your main areas of interest. You can look for other related areas and improve your knowledge of them, building on your existing expertise. On your bonus CD there is a product finder worksheet that will help you narrow your interests and get related product ideas.

b. Start choosing products to sell

Now that you have an idea of what kind of thing you want to sell on, you can start looking for something specific. Make a list of your top five interests, hobbies, or passions. Write them across the top of a piece of paper, and underneath each write down 5-10 related products. The more specific the product is the better. Now that you've come up with a few product ideas, you need to determine if there is a demand for any of your ideas. We'll show you tools and techniques that will reveal the answers.

B. Researching Markets

If there's one thing that separates the professional sellers from the beginners, it's market research. Smart sellers don't even think about stocking up on inventory unless they already know there are people willing to buy it. There are two kinds of research -

a. Proactive

Proactive research helps you find profitable products to sell. You use this type of research to find a niche market with high demand and low supply, where you can make the most profits. Proactive research is market based, you start by searching categories and trends for a niche market that's not being served and finding out how those people find what they're looking for. This type of research makes predictions about what will sell. It starts with broad categories and you dig to find viable markets within specific categories.

The Category Listings show all the items currently for sale on eBay, sorted by category. This page gives you an overview of the entire eBay marketplace, it contains a list of all the categories in which items on eBay are listed. You can also see the number of items being sold in each category, which can give you an idea of that category's popularity. Within this page you can click a category and view all of the subcategories. Every category on eBay has a number of subcategories and the further down you dig, the more specific these subcategories become.

As you dig down through eBay's categories and exploring different products, you'll want to analyze the categories. Pay attention so you can -

- Find out how many listings exist in a particular category
- Assess the demand within categories
- Check out the level of competition within categories
- See how well individual items sell within their categories

An "All Categories" search that digs down into the subcategories is a quick and easy way to get a snapshot of the eBay marketplace at any particular time. If you're just starting out, your best bet is to select two or three categories that you find particularly interesting and do some digging around to see what products are out there. If you already have a few items to sell, choose the most appropriate category for them and start your digging there. Click on the category and subcategory you're interested in. In Preferences click Completed Listings, then can check individual listings to learn -

- The number of bids
- The amounts bid or most common fixed price
- How the sellers write their titles and product descriptions

This isn't just information, it's insight into who your main competitors are at any particular time and how successful their auctions are. If you examine other sellers' listings, you'll start to understand what works and what doesn't on eBay and in individual categories.

b. Reactive research

Reactive research helps you decide how you'll sell a particular item. You use this type of research to narrow your market down to a niche, and find exact data on an item's sales history. This will give you all the information you need to decide whether you should sell that item or find a different one, and to decide how you'll approach selling the item. Reactive research is product based, it looks at sales histories and trends of specific items to find out how those items have sold in the past and whether you can make a profit selling them. Use the viable products spreadsheet on your bonus disc and use it to keep track of the information you find and the results you get.

a. View completed listings

Viewing past auctions lets you see the all-important final selling price of an item, helping you understand potential profit margins. It lets you see an auction's bidding history, which lets you gauge an item's popularity. Here's how to find the final selling price -

- Click the Advanced Search link next to the search box.
- Enter your search words and any other specific criteria, such as a particular category.
- Click the checkbox marked Completed listings
- Hit the Search button

A completed listing of an item that you have for sale is a treasure trove of research information. Sort the list by price and you can view the final selling price of items. Look at how many bids were placed on each item. This is important when trying to determine if there is enough interest in the item. Sort the results by end date so you can see what days successful auctions ended. Learn how to sell similar items by studying how other, more experienced sellers do it. Learn from other sellers' mistakes by checking out listings that didn't sell. These listings including unsold items and items that sold for a low price or attracted few bids can teach you just as much as more successful auctions can.

You can also use the Completed Listings option to search for a rival seller's completed auctions. Just browse to an auction being run by that seller, click View seller's other auctions, and then check the Completed Listings button to search for specific items sold by that person. Checking out the listings of previously sold and unsold items is essential when you're deciding what you should sell.

b. Use "Want It Now"

One sign that your product has potential is if people want it but can't find it. Want It Now is a classified ad area of eBay that allows buyers to post ads for items they want to purchase. eBay sellers can then respond to these ads with their products for sale. Here's how it works -

- An eBay member places a short ad for an item they want to buy.
- The ad appears on a list of wanted items that are grouped into the same categories that eBay uses on its main auction pages.
- Sellers browse these listings and respond to individual ads, either by

creating an auction page containing the item that a buyer is looking for, or by notifying the buyer that they are already running an auction for that item.

- The buyer then bids on the item.

For buyers, the advantage is that they can save time searching for something they want. For sellers, it's an opportunity to see if someone is looking for a specific item that you have for sale, and to assess demand for items you're thinking of selling. People usually post items in want it now because they've already searched and can't find them anywhere else, it's a great place to find markets that aren't being served.

C. <u>Free research resources</u>

Here are four ways to get valuable information from eBay -

a. eBay Pulse

eBay Pulse shows you the current top eBay stores by number of active listings. Check them out to see what they're selling and how they're selling it. Try buying a couple of cheap things from these stores to check out their customer service, packaging, delivery times, and how they do things. You can view the top 10 keywords and watched listings for each category and subcategory.

b. Popular products

On the Popular Products page, you can view the products with the largest number of current listings on eBay. Click a category like DVDs, Video Games, or Fiction Books and you'll see lists of thousands of items in order of popularity. When you're considering whether or not to sell a particular item on eBay, make sure to go to this page to check out its popularity first.

c. Popular keywords

eBay Keywords will become more useful when it comes to optimizing your listings, so people find them but they also give you an idea of what products eBay shoppers are searching for. You can also browse the most popular keywords that people use to search eBay.

d. Other eBayers

Check out the Community Hub to learn how you can communicate with other eBayers, ask questions, and join discussion groups relating to products you're interested in selling. You'll find a real community out there that can help you find a market and get some more ideas. Forums can be good if you have an idea of what you want to sell and you find someone who is willing to share their experiences.

D. Paid research resources

There are a number of third-party tools available for you to use to handle many of the tasks involved in managing an eBay business, including listing and managing your auctions. Some of these are very good market research tools that you can use to determine the best selling opportunities on eBay. eBay offers a lot of useful free resources and information to help with your market research but they don't go to the same level of depth that will be useful to you. These third-party research tools are available for monthly or yearly fees. They all take their data from eBay auctions and give you a lot of great information. This allows you to build your market knowledge that much quicker.

a. Terapeak

Terapeak is an online suite of research tools starting at $24.95 a month, with yearly discounts available. Terapeak lets you do keyword searches on eBay auctions completed in the last 90 days. You can browse all the categories and dig down into subcategories to find details of listings, competing sellers, trends, and individual auctions. The software is Web based, so all you need is a computer with Internet access and a browser. Using Terapeak, you can find out how different listing features affect an auction. You can search for items that used the specific combination of features you may be considering using in your auctions.

Terapeak contains numerous graphs and information charts that show you things like the best days to end auctions and the most effective auction durations. By default, Terapeak draws data exclusively from eBay.com, but there are options for eBay's international sites such as eBay UK, Germany, Australia, France, and Canada. The Trends tab in Terapeak is great for seeing how the popularity of an item fluctuates over a year. This will help you spot any regular and seasonal trends you can take advantage of by stocking up during the lows and ramping up your listings when they peak.

b. HammerTap

HammerTap offers a free 10-day trial of their Analysis tool, during which you can download and use the software to research the eBay market. If you decide to continue using it, it'll cost you $19.95 per month. You can search for items and auctions across three areas - eBay Auction, eBay Seller, and eBay Category. Within each area you can search complete categories or auctions using specific keywords. You can view the results of up to 10,000 auctions and sort them by title, number of bids, starting price, fees, and type of auction to find the most successful and profitable auctions.

You can use this information to research products you think might sell on eBay and find out if anyone else is having any success with them. You can also get the lowdown on your competitors' auctions, and work out the profit margins by seeing what each item sold for. Before deciding how much you should spend on your listings, check out the Insertion Fees column that lets you see how much each listing cost in eBay fees and see what effect, if any, extra paid-for features have on the final selling price of an item. This the software that we use and it has greatly helped increase our sales on eBay.

c. Vendio

Vendio is an online suite of research and sales tools. Vendio's eBay research tools cost $20 per month, and include "clustering technology" that eliminates most irrelevant results.

5. Analyze Your Competition

A. <u>Investigate</u>

The easiest way to start looking for your competition is to do a series of keyword searches on eBay using the words and phrases that your customers would use to find you. Look on Store Search as well to see what the big guys are doing. Then take a look at the results. What other listings are showing up for those keywords? Those are the ones you need to keep your eye on. Once you've found some sellers listing items similar to yours, do a Completed Listings search. To do that, you'll need to use the Advanced Search page and click the checkbox that says Completed Listings Only.

Now you're looking at the listings that sold for the most money. Where do your listings rank? Are there lots of sellers who are getting more money selling items similar to yours, or just a few? While you're looking for listings similar to yours, keep track of your actual competitors. Look for the sellers with great feedback ratings and a large number of completed listings, and write down their Seller IDs. You might want to buy some items from your top-selling competitors to see how they manage their sales process.

There's only so much you can learn about your competitors and your market by checking out the Completed Listings. To get the important details, you're going to use the tools you used to investigate markets to investigate your competitors. Want to learn what your competition is doing wrong? Check out the <u>Toolhaus</u> Negative/Neutral Feedback Tool. This tool lets you take a closer look at all the Negative and Neutral Feedback your competition receives on eBay and see all the feedback they've left for others.

B. <u>Get the details</u>

You've done your research into listings similar to yours, now it's time to dig a little deeper into the people posting those listings. Competition research is a necessary step in researching a viable market. Careful research allows you confirm whether a viable market exists. Here's how to perform competition research -

- Go to eBay and type the name of an item you're researching into the search box.
- Scroll down on the results page of active listings, under the yellow navigation bar on the left to the Matching eBay Stores area.
- Click See all matching eBay Stores. This will indicate which sellers have the highest quantity of that item. They are your biggest competitors due to

the volume of active core listings they have!

- Click the top one and work your way down the list following these steps.
- Once at the seller's eBay store, click their first listing.
- Once in the listing, find the section on the right-hand side titled Meet the Seller and click the List link next to View seller's other items.
- On that page, type the name of the item again in the search box just above the listings. eBay will now perform a search for that item only within that seller's listings.
- After receiving the results, observe how many active auctions they have for that item and proceed to check Completed Listings on the left yellow navigation bar, under search options. Click the Show Items button at the bottom of the navigation bar.

The results are now the completed listings for this seller for the past 14 days for that specific item. Observe their sell-through rate and other interesting details. Once you've taken some notes, click one of the listings. In the Meet the Seller section in the upper right corner, you can review that seller's eBay profile to get some insight into who they are. As you review the seller, also analyze their listings for the item in question. Look for successful listing strategies they have implemented, or areas where you think their listings could be better. Look at elements such as their titles, descriptions, pictures, listing durations, auction types, payment methods, shipping destinations, etc. Looking behind a competitor's cashier counter using eBay is a start. Using a tool like Hammertap will give you great insight into how to compete with them.

6. Your Profit Margin

A. <u>Fees affect profits</u>

You may think you don't have to worry about pricing items in advance if they're going to be put up for auction. Knowing the price your items are likely to sell for will help you calculate how much you can spend on buying your stock and on eBay's listing fees. When any of the major offline auction houses like Sotheby's or Christie's sell items at auction, they typically take between 10 and 20% of the sale price as a brokerage fee. eBay doesn't take quite that much. Iif you want your business to remain profitable, it's essential you know exactly how much eBay does charge.

The two charges you need to be aware of are Insertion fees and Final Value fees. These are the two unavoidable eBay fees -

a. Insertion fees

These are the basic fees you'll pay to create your auction listing. They're based on your starting price and/or listing format. A quick look at eBay's fee table should tell you why so many items get started at $0.99 -- because it costs $0.15 - $0.20 less per item than starting it at $1. Check the eBay fees page for the cost of listing items. Think of your insertion fee as insurance. If you want to sell an expensive camera for at least $50 and not risk losing it for a buck, you can pay $2 and start it at $50. Starting it at $0.99 will certainly make people notice. You'll get some bargain-hunters watching your listing and maybe they'll even start a bidding frenzy. Test these strategies with some lower-priced items and find out what works best for you.

b. Final value fee

This is the second unavoidable fee. The only way you can avoid paying this one is if your item doesn't sell and you don't want that to happen. Final Value fees are based on what your item sells for, the higher the sale price, the higher the fee. The more you pay, the better it is for you. Check the eBay fees page for the final value fee of items.

In June 2009, eBay kicked off its new 5 Free Insertion Fees Every 30 Days campaign. No matter what the starting price, you pay no Insertion Fees on your first five auction-style listings every month when you use eBay's Sell Your Item or Simple listing form. If your items don't sell, you pay nothing. All other auctions after the first five will revert to the regular Insertion Fee and Current Value fee system.

If those five items sell, you pay a flat rate of 8.75% of the final value or $20, whichever is lower. Many sellers are complaining that this new format is forcing them to pay more money than they do under the regular fee structure. You can avoid paying these extra fees. If you ensure that your first five auctions are for items that will either sell for less than $25, or more than $500, you will save money. These five free insertion fees don't work if you use automated software such as eBay's Turbolister or a third-party tool such as Auctiva to manage your auctions. So if your auctions fall into the safe area of less than $25 or more than $500, don't use the software. If they don't, then use it for every listing.

To guarantee you don't end up spending more than necessary on your listing fees, always calculate exactly what your final value fees will end up costing you by using a tool such as this eBay and PayPal Fee Calculator. A few seconds of research could end up saving you a lot of money in the long run. Fees are charged to your Seller Account for every item you sell.

B. Calculate your profit margins

Understanding your profit margins, how much money you make on each sale, is crucial to making money on eBay. This is a basic formula for working out the profit margin -

Profit = Gross Income - Cost

Your profits are whatever is left over after you take your costs into account. You then need to know how to calculate your gross income and your costs.

Gross Income = Item Final Selling Price + Shipping & Handling Fee

Cost = Item Purchase Cost + Listing fees + Final Value fees + PayPal or Credit Card fees + Shipping costs

Here's an example of that formula in action - Say you list a book that you bought at a flea market for $2. You go with a starting price of 99 cents, and charge $5 for shipping and handling. The winning bid is $10, and your buyer pays you using PayPal.

Your Gross Income is the final selling price - $10 + $5 = $15

Your Costs are more complicated -

- Item purchase cost - $2.00

- Listing fee - $0.10
- Final value fee - $10 final sale price, $0.88
- PayPal fee - $0.75
- Shipping costs - $4.00

So your total costs are: $2.00 + $0.10 + $0.88 + $0.75 + $4.00 = $7.73

Subtract your Costs from your Gross Income: $15.00 - $7.73 = $7.27 profit

There are a lot of factors involved in working out your final profit for a sale. For help with your math, try the free eBay fee calculator we suggested. You can edit certain numbers and the calculator is updated regularly as eBay's fees change. Now that you understand how profit is calculated, there are things you can do to increase your profit margins -

- Increase your final selling price
- Increase your S&H fees (overcharging for S&H will decrease the visibility of your listing in searches)
- Decrease your item purchase cost
- Decrease your eBay listing fees
- Decrease your final value fees
- Decrease your credit card fees
- Decrease your shipping costs

There are advantages and disadvantages to each of these strategies. Some are easier said than done and others may affect your auction negatively, which is why you must always test a strategy before going full speed ahead with it.

C. Selling styles

When it comes to deciding between selling lots of low-priced items or fewer high-priced items, you must take a careful look at your profit margins.

a. Low-price, high-volume items

Many eBay sellers go the low-price, high-volume route and focus on turning over a lot of stock as quickly as possible. To do this you need good, reliable suppliers. You also need to stay on top of all the extra work involved in listing lots of auctions and shipping lots of items. There are a couple of ways you can get around the extra workload needed to sell large quantities of low-priced items. Try making up groups of similar items and selling them in packages. A big consideration when selling large volumes of lower-priced items is that the profit margin can be very small due to the costs incurred through eBay and PayPal or credit card fees.

When you're doing your market research, sort the results of your searches for particular items by price and see what the average prices are in categories that interest you. By adding the fees to the average price, you can calculate your profit margin on selling in lots versus selling items individually.

b. High-price, low-volume items

Selling high-priced items at lower volumes looks like an attractive option for eBay sellers. There are all kinds of high-priced items for sale on eBay. Selling high-priced items generally means you need to sell fewer of them to make money. Your success with this strategy depends on your profit margin. You still have to be able to buy your stock at a low price so you can mark it up enough to make a decent profit. Selling high-priced items on eBay can be more difficult than selling items of lower value. You need to make sure that your product descriptions are accurate and comprehensive to avoid any negative Feedback from buyers who find something wrong with them.

There's often a smaller market for high-priced items, which means fewer people for you to sell to. Although good customer service is vital when selling any item, it's especially important when selling more expensive products. People are spending a lot of money and are putting their faith in you and your business. They are trusting you to deliver the item to them in the condition you say it's in. You also need to take particular care when packaging, insuring, and shipping expensive items, including making international buyers aware that they will be responsible for any duties and customs fees.

c. Start low and aim high

Selling low-priced items is a good way for new eBayers to start out. There's less risk involved and it's usually easier to package, ship, and store low-priced items, which means you're less likely to have unhappy customers who leave you negative feedback. You can also build your feedback rating and DSRs quickly by selling more items more frequently as long as you do a good job of it. Once you have more experience selling on eBay, it's worth exploring opportunities to sell high-priced items, assuming you can buy stock at low enough prices to guarantee yourself a profit. You effectively make your money when you buy stock, buying at a low price is just as vital as selling at a high price. This is especially true when it comes to selling in highly competitive, hot markets. Whichever pricing strategy you go for, remember to focus on what makes you the best profit margins.

D. <u>Your shipping process</u>

Shipping is one of the biggest costs of doing business on eBay and it's one of the biggest sources of negative Feedback as well as being the DSR category that gets the lowest scores. With a little bit of preparation and some smart shipping strategies, you can streamline your shipping process.

a. Get shipping essentials for the lowest price

Having your supplies on hand will increase your shipping efficiency. Getting the best possible price for them will translate into higher profits. You don't need to spend tons on shipping supplies if you know where to look. Here are a few tricks -

- Ask for freebies from your courier or post office
- Use recycled materials
- Buy inexpensive supplies on eBay

Once you've got your supply sources, create a special work area where you will store all of your shipping supplies and prepare all of your packaging.

b. Online shipping labels

If you're facing long lines in the post office, here are a few tips to help -

- Buy a postal scale
- Print shipping labels online
- Sign up for corporate accounts to save money

Now that you have a shipping system, you'll be rewarded with higher profits and more time to spend creating listings and sourcing products. You'll also encourage positive Feedback and great DSRs from pleased buyers who receive your packages fast for the lowest price.

c. Bonus from PayPal

You've signed up with PayPal, so it makes sense to tell your bidders that you'd like them to use it. PayPal will pay you to. Here's how to set up "PayPal Preferred" for your eBay auctions -

- On your Account Overview page, click the Profile tab.
- Under Selling Preferences, click Auctions.
- On the Auction Accounts page, under PayPal Preferred on eBay, click On/Off.

Once you've turned this option on, a PayPal Preferred message is inserted in the View Item page and in the Choose Payment Method page of all your eBay listings. With PayPal Preferred on your eBay listing or your website, you qualify to earn 1% cash back on every purchase you make with your PayPal ATM/debit card.

E. Account for all costs

It's easy for new sellers on eBay to get caught up in the excitement of finding products, creating auction listings, and making sales. Not paying attention to the costs involved in the process. Some of these costs are easy to determine but what about the time you spend finding, storing, packing, and shipping that item? As well as tracking all the costs involved with the auction process, it's important to know the value of your item. There are many instances where unknowing sellers have sold collectibles or antiques for much less than market value because they didn't do the research to discover what the item was worth.

a. Understand the hidden costs

When purchasing inventory to resell on eBay you need to keep track of how much time you spend shopping for and gathering the items. If you were shopping online, how many hours did you spend in front of the computer? The real cost of acquisition is often much more than people think. Running an eBay business is time consuming. If you don't keep a close eye on how many hours you're spending on it, there's a chance you'll end up working for less than minimum wage.

b. Your product's true value

In addition to understanding all the costs involved with selling your merchandise on eBay, it's important that you know the true value of any item you're selling. If you don't know what your product is worth, there's a good chance you won't get the highest price possible. Check out other online auction sites. You may be surprised to find out there are online auction sites devoted to almost every subject you can imagine. Trying to find information on these auction sites may be a little bit more difficult than it is on eBay but with some searching you'll find pricing information.

The only way you're going to know for certain what buyers will pay for your product is to test. Try out different pricing strategies to see which one yields the highest returns. Keep tweaking your sales process to continually improve your profits. A great technique to prove to bidders the value of your item is to include photographs of any name brand tags, inscriptions, or markings. It's important to realize that a good photo of a valuable inscription or tag could be worth hundreds of dollars.

Not understanding all your costs is a prescription for disaster in any business. Before deciding whether or not to sell an item on eBay you need to know all the costs involved. Hard expenses such as eBay's insertion and final value fees are easy to determine, but don't forget to take into consideration hidden costs such as the time you spent acquiring the merchandise you're planning to sell. Over time, you'll gain experience and have a better idea of how much you can get for an item on eBay especially if you specialize in a certain type of product. Once you become an expert, it's easy to stay on top of market and pricing trends.

7. Sourcing Ideas

A. <u>Become an expert buyer</u>

The best way to ensure that you're getting the best prices available is to become an expert in one or more product areas. If you have knowledge about a certain product line, it becomes easy to spot deals because you know the true value of different items. You don't need to be a leading authority on any subject just yet but you do need to start somewhere. When you're trying to find some items to sell on eBay, keep your eyes open for any deal you think is good, and keep these tips in mind -

- Start small
- Concentrate on three or four types of product
- Never stop learning about what you sell
- Be a disciplined buyer
- Build lasting relationships with your best suppliers
- Talk to everyone about what you're looking for

Becoming an expert in one or more product areas will take some time, but you'll be rewarded for your efforts. It will be much easier for you to stay on top of market and pricing trends. You'll write more powerful item descriptions and be able to distinguish yourself from competitors. Here's a list of places to source products to sell on eBay -

a. Source locally

After cleaning out their own and their familie's basements with the help of eBay auctions, many sellers start scouring local sources. For many people the thrill of the chase is exciting. Don't forget to find real bargains consistently; you'll need to have done your homework. As long as you've researched a few different markets, understand your costs, and know what items are selling for you should have no problem finding a few deals to get yourself started. You'd surprised at how little most people know about the true value of many items. Here are a few different options to consider when sourcing close to your home –

- Friends and family
- Garage and yard sales
- Flea markets
- Swap meets
- Thrift stores
- Retail stores
- Club stores and discount retailers
- Trade shows

- Craft fairs
- Salvage and junk yards
- Local liquidations

b. Source at other auctions

In addition to eBay, there are tons of online and offline auctions that can be excellent sources of items to sell on eBay -

- Police auctions
- Government auctions
- Estate sales
- eBay, Here are some buying secrets that can help you find some great deals – Find items that are being sold poorly, Find sellers who don't know the value of an item, Find auctions that end at awkward times
- Bid late
- Other online auctions

Because eBay is the big kid on the block, the selling prices on other online auction sites are generally lower.

c. Source new products to sell

Most of the product sources we've been discussing so far are good places to find used or secondhand items. If you plan to sell new products on eBay, you'll have to come up with different ways to find your inventory. The good news is there are still plenty of options available –

- Drop shippers
- Wholesalers
- Online liquidators
- Buy from the manufacturer

d. Other sourcing ideas

You've learned about sourcing used products locally and through other auctions, and about multiple sources of new products. Let's look at some other possibilities that don't fall into any particular category -

- Seasonal selling
- Free stuff
- Classified ads
- Want ads

- Develop your own products
- Sell a service, You only want to consider selling a service on eBay if, You're an expert in something that you can promote online, You sometimes experience slow periods with your regular eBay auctions and want another stream of revenue, You don't want to deal with the storage, packing, and shipping tasks involved in selling physical products.
- Sell to other eBay Sellers
- Sell bundles of items
- Customize items
- Novelty / weird items
- Sell local merchandise to the rest of the world
- Trading assistant program

B. Drop ship

Drop shipping is when you are responsible for selling an item and the manufacturer or distributor ships it to your customers. This means you can sell quality, brand-name products on eBay for a profit, while someone else looks after product development and order fulfillment. This is a great arrangement for a number of reasons. It saves you the cost of building your own inventory. If you're like most people starting out on eBay, you don't have a ton of extra money lying around and the last thing you want to do is tie up your cash in inventory that you may or may not be able to sell.

No inventory means no leftovers. If the product you sell suddenly becomes outdated, obsolete, or uncool, you aren't the one with a warehouse full of stock nobody will buy. Many eBayers find themselves having to offer deep discounts and taking losses just to get old products out of their homes or warehouses to make room for more inventory. You'll be able to sell brand-new products almost instantly. Since you don't have to worry about stocking inventory, if you find that your customers are clamoring for a particular product, you can start listing auctions for the item in just a few days.

Even with all of the benefits associated with using drop shippers, you need to think carefully before deciding to adopt this business model -

- Back-ordered products - Drop-shipping companies occasionally run out of product, which can be devastating to a seller. Bidders usually assume that the items they are bidding on are in your possession and ready to ship. Long delays will be reflected in your DSRs.

- Fees - Some drop shippers charge sign-up fees ranging from $25 and up, just for the right to sell their products. You also get a processing fee for sending the item to your customer. When you combine these fees with eBay and PayPal expenses, there can be very little profit left over for you.

- Loss of control over customer service - By deciding to use drop shippers, you have lost control of certain elements of your customer service.

- Volume discounts - It's hard to find quality drop shippers that cater to small sellers. Most look for large volume buyers that move a ton of merchandise. If you approach them with small orders, it will be difficult to negotiate a decent price.

These drawbacks can be overcome, there are plenty of eBay sellers earning money with drop shipping. You simply need to be aware of the potential hazards. There's one more downside to drop shipping – SCAMS. With the rising popularity of drop shipping, many scams have also risen around the industry. There are fake lists of drop shippers on offer for hundreds of dollars online. Don't let these scammers scare you away. Be aware that they exist, and always look twice at any company before agreeing to go into a business with them.

When it comes to selling on eBay, it's better to own what you sell, and never leave your customer service and therefore your feedback rating in the hands of others. There are a couple of reputable drop shipping resources we recommend -

- Worldwide Brands (http://www.worldwidebrands.com/) - Offers a directory of legitimate drop shippers and Worldwide Brands is also the only eBay-certified publisher of drop ship and wholesale product sourcing information on the Internet.

- Doba (http://www.doba.com/) - Gives you immediate access to millions wholesale products all in one place. By combining the purchasing power of all its members, Doba offers lower wholesale prices and significantly reduced, or eliminated, drop ship fees. Doba offers a free 7-Day trial.

C. Wholesalers

Wholesalers can be very profitable sources of products if you buy low and sell high, but you must do your research and choose carefully. One of the secrets to success on eBay is finding reliable sources of products at low prices, but, when it comes to buying wholesale, it's not as easy as just calling up a wholesale company and starting to list auctions on eBay. Wholesale is constantly misunderstood. It's not some magical bargain-basement price available to anyone who can find the email address; it's a relative term based mostly on how much of a particular item you are able to purchase.

Many sellers think that by finding a legitimate wholesale supplier, they will instantly be able to sell products for less than anyone else on eBay. This doesn't take into account that they have to compete with other sellers who might have more buying power and get even better discounts. When you see products being sold on eBay for less than you can purchase them wholesale, the other seller more than likely bought thousands of units to get that great deal.

Unless you use a service like Doba you'll have to look in niche categories and build a relationship with the wholesalers you find. If you're successful, eventually you can start purchasing in larger quantities and get the low wholesale prices you need to out-compete others in your niche. You should start looking locally first. Local wholesalers will be quicker, and you can potentially save money on shipping and customs paperwork. If you're using a search engine, you'll have the best luck if you type the name of your item along with these keywords -

- Wholesale
- Wholesaler
- Wholesalers
- Distributor
- Discount
- Importer
- Reseller
- Factory Authorized
- Manufacturer
- Wholesale Distributor

For best results, include the region, city, or town you're in to the above terms to narrow your search results. Another resource you can use is your local Chamber of Commerce, which can put you in touch with distributors and wholesalers within your area. However you find them, before you start doing business with a wholesaler make sure you've done your due diligence. Research the company, get references, and be extra cautious when you're dealing with companies outside of your own country. Here are a few of the best wholesalers -

- goWholesale
- Wholesale Central
- Worldwide Brands
- Doba

Don't forget to check out the list of wholesalers and drop shippers on your bonus CD.

D. Liquidation sales

Products often remain unsold for reasons unrelated to their quality. Perfectly good products might wind up in a bargain bin because they're seasonal items, last year's models, or customer returns. Products that other retailers are in a hurry to get rid of can be perfect for your business. Try visiting liquidation companies or stores that are hosting one-time liquidation sales to look for these kinds of items -

- Seasonal goods
- Last year's models.
- Customer returns
- Overstock
- Discontinued items

The best way to find liquidators locally is to check your phone book. Some cities have dedicated liquidation outlets too, like Liquidation World or you can try Liquidation.com to find surplus inventory available in bulk lots. Online, visit a search engine and try a search with keywords like -

- Liquidation
- Bankruptcy sale
- Overstock
- Clearance
- Truckload sales
- Excess inventory
- b2b auctions
- Salvage items
- Surplus

The main disadvantage of liquidation stock as a sourcing strategy is that the products are usually one-time purchases. That means it's difficult to rely on these sources for a constant supply of inventory that falls within your areas of expertise. This doesn't mean you should completely ignore products outside your areas of expertise. Just keep in mind that long-term success is usually the result of an inexpensive and consistent supply of merchandise.

Do your research to see if there is a demand for any products you're thinking of buying, and work out your likely profit margins. Be aware that to get the best deals, you must pick up the phone and build relationships with wholesalers and retail outlets. Always ask anyone you're dealing with if they have any merchandise they want to liquidate. If you don't ask, they won't tell you.

8. Contacting Suppliers

A. Create a good first impression

Once you've identified reputable wholesalers you'd like to do business with, now you need to prove you're a legitimate business they would want to do business with. To start, you must set up a legal business and position yourself as an online retailer. Legitimate suppliers can only do business with retailers who can legally buy wholesale at least in the US. These websites can provide information on how to do this in the US -

- The American Institute of Certified Public Accountants
- U.S. Small Business Administration

If you are in another country, you can easily find information online about obtaining a business license by visiting government websites. Once you're set up as a legitimate business, you'll have a company name but naming your business is just the start you should go further to show how professional you are. Here are a few additional steps you can take to ensure that your business has a positive, professional image -

- Set up a web page that showcases your business
- Purchase a domain name and set up a business email address
- Set up business voicemail
- Use a business letterhead and get business cards printed
- Join business associations such as your local Chamber of Commerce

All this helps you to create a professional image that will help when it comes to negotiating deals to buy products from wholesalers.

B. Impress sources

The key thing to remember when contacting wholesalers or manufacturers is be prepared. It means doing some research up front before contacting them -

- Find out the basic requirements of each wholesaler
- Set up an account with wholesalers
- Request a product catalog
- Research the wholesaler's company history
- Decide how you want to present your company to them

Take the time to learn about and understand the wholesalers you plan to contact.

Visit their websites and take notes. Not only will they be impressed with the depth of your knowledge about their company but you'll feel more confident in negotiations with them. Be prepared to contact a supplier many times before they'll agree to do a deal with you. If they ask questions you don't know the answers to, it's okay to tell them you'll have to get back to them with the answer.

Multiple contacts show you're serious and can be a great way to build up a good relationship with a supplier. Building a good relationship will allow you to find out about the best deals and negotiate better pricing. For best results, contact a variety of suppliers. Ideally you should contact new suppliers on a regular basis, finding at least a couple of new ones each week until you have a solid list of resources. It's a good idea to set up a supplier file to track the ones you've contacted and log the outcome of each contact. Don't forget to request a product catalog from every supplier. If you don't get the result you want, you can always try again later. When you've done your research and are ready to make contact, here are some helpful tips that will improve your chances of making a deal.

When contacting suppliers by phone -

- Before you call, practice your "professional" voice. Call as the "buyer" for your company and keep your introduction brief and to the point, using the phrase "our company" and "we" instead of "my company" and "I."
- Be prepared with information about your budget, the products you're interested in, your payment methods, and anything else a supplier might need. It's a good idea to have all this information at your fingertips, whether that means writing it down on 3x5 index cards or typing it into your word processor so you can refer to your screen during the call
- Take control of the phone call by asking the questions you prepared in advance, but don't just stick to a script, listen to what the vendor says and tailor your questions accordingly. People can always tell if you're reading from a script, and most of them don't like it

When contacting suppliers by email -

- Do not use a free service such as Gmail, Yahoo Mail, or Hotmail it looks amateurish and will not get you a deal. Instead, buy a domain name that includes your company name and set up an email address at that domain.
- Create a basic one-page website for your business that the suppliers you contact can click through to, and always include a link to that site in your email signature

When contacting suppliers through their website -

- Wholesalers get a lot of inquiries through their online forms, so keep your correspondence brief and to the point. Don't ask too many questions, just ask your most important question in the form, and save all your other questions for your follow-up

When contacting suppliers through postal mail -

- Always use your business letterhead
- Ensure you are sending your letters to the appropriate contacts at the wholesalers' companies. In your letter, let them know that you are writing because you are interested in retailing their products.
- Follow up all mail correspondence with a phone call

When contacting suppliers in person -

- Call in advance and make an appointment
- Build a good, profitable, working relationship with your potential supplier with face-to-face communication
- Don't forget business cards

C. Questions and common objections

Questions to always ask -

- Do you have a product catalog you can send to us?
- Do you have a price list you can give us?
- Is there a minimum quantity when ordering products?
- Can you send us a sample? We are willing to pay for one.
- Do you have an email "special offer" list we can get on?
- What shipping options do you provide?
- What are your ordering processes?
- What are your shipping terms?
- What are the lead and delivery times for orders?
- Who is the best person to contact?

Things you should never say -

- I work from home.
- I am an eBay seller.
- I don't have enough money for the minimum order.
- I want to negotiate better pricing.

If you follow these guidelines, you can't go wrong. The key thing is to stay professional at all times and convince suppliers that you will be able to sell their products effectively. Wholesalers will not necessarily be falling over themselves to take your business, so you should take steps to prevent any objections in the first place, and know how to overcome them if something does come up. To prevent objections, do not volunteer too much information initially. Keep your questions brief and to the point, and if you find an objection is being repeated from wholesaler to wholesaler, rework your approach.

If a supplier does seem unwilling to do business with you, make sure that their objection is specific. For instance, if they say, "We don't do business with small retailers," turn that question around and ask them, "What volume of business would we need to do with you in order to set up an account?" Do not argue with a supplier. Instead, gather information and see if there is a way to eventually meet their requirements. If a supplier requires you to have a website and you don't have one, thank them for their time, create a website, and contact them again a couple of months later.

Some suppliers will not do business with online retailers no matter what. If a supplier is firm about this, don't waste your time trying to change their policy, move on and try another supplier. Your business should be much bigger in six months time, so a supplier who doesn't want to deal with you today might be willing to deal with you in six months time.

Chapter Two

Create Listings that Raise your Profits

1. Add Great Photos to your Listings

A. <u>Enhance listings with photos</u>

Items listed with photos attract more bidders and higher bids. That means better pictures equals better sell-through rates, and more pictures almost always mean more profits. The main drawback for people who bid and buy on eBay is that they can't physically inspect or handle the item they're thinking about purchasing. No number of images in your product description is going to change that. You can make sure that your prospective bidders have as complete a picture as possible. A badly lit, out-of-focus, and unappealing pictures happen every day on eBay. All those poor-quality photos represent a great opportunity for you, by spending just a few minutes on your product images, you can make your items stand out from the crowd and attract more bids for your auctions. When it comes to incorporating images into your product description, your product images need to reinforce and enhance the words you're using to describe and sell your item. Images that back up everything you say and show your item in its best light will generate more bids and higher value bids, ultimately leading to higher final values for your products. A good set of images of your item will -

- Reinforce your credibility
- Increase the item's desirability
- Help bidders make an informed decision
- Attract more bids
- Gain the trust of your bidders
- Help you score high Item Description DSRs

The number of images you use for each item depends on its value and whether you are paying for eBay to host the images or not. A higher-value or more unusual item needs more images to show it off in its best light or address any questions bidders may have. The higher price makes it worthwhile to provide these extra shots, even if you have to pay for them. You've seen enough listings to know that images really do make a difference and you've done enough research to prove it.

Look at the listings and listing promotions of top sellers you've been studying. Almost every time, listings with good-quality photos outperform those without. More detail is better than less and Gallery photos are essential, especially in categories with a lot of competition. Some of the images should be designed to show off the item, such as close-ups of an interesting or unusual detail on an item of vintage clothing. Other images should aim to verify that what you are saying about the item in your product description is true. You can also use images to address common concerns that may exist in the marketplace about your particular item.

A single good product image is often enough for a low-value item. The amount of time and effort you put into an auction should correspond to the value of the item you're selling. When running your own eBay business, time is money. Try to include as many images as it takes to showcase your items and enhance your product descriptions, especially if you're hosting the images yourself to save on eBay fees. Good images are one of the drivers of high bids in eBay auctions. You don't need a room of high-tech camera equipment or a degree in photography to take effective product shots. A digital camera and a little know-how can produce professional-looking shots that enhance your product descriptions and encourage more people to place higher bids on your auctions.

a. Various angles

It's impossible for bidders to pick up your item and examine it closely. You can give them the same experience by taking photos of your item from various angles, allowing them to see the whole picture. With eBay's Picture Services, extra photos are .15 cents each or around $1.00 - $1.50 you can get the Picture Pack, which gives you up to 12 photos and Supersize. If you go with a third-party auction management software company, you can find plans that allow for unlimited pictures and bulk image hosting.

b. Get close

You should always give your bidders an image showing the whole item you're selling. You should include pictures with as much close-up detail as possible of significant features, such as the lens of a camera, the pattern on a china plate, and so on. It's important to show any imperfections in close-up shots. Be up-front about any faults with your item.

c. Light images well

To showcase your items you need to make sure bidders can see them clearly. That means lighting them properly, instead of just relying on your flash to light your subject. Depending on the size of your items, you can easily set up a small studio in a corner of your bedroom or home office, with a little practice you'll find you can take clear, well-lit images every time. You don't need a lot of expensive equipment to light your items properly, to get good natural lighting in your photographs, and better color quality, take your pictures outdoors. An overcast but not gloomy day will provide the best results. Bright sunny days are not as good for photos, the light is too harsh.

d. Remove flash glare

It's better not to use your flash at all because it leads to glare and unnatural coloring. If you're stuck with a flash, you can avoid flash glare if you understand how it works. Flash glare is caused by the light from your flash being reflected off your subject straight back into the lens of your camera. If you want to avoid the glare, you need it to bounce off the object at an angle. Then the light won't go straight back to the lens.

e. Prop up or scan flat items

If you're photographing flat items and need to stand them up on end but don't want to hold the item with one hand and try to take a photo with the other, it's worth buying a small plate stand to keep them upright. It will hold the item up for you, as well as tilt it so you avoid flash glare.

f. Contextual reference

If the size of your product is something that may be important to bidders, include another item in your shot to help bidders gauge the size of the item.

g. Color reference

If the color of an item is an important selling point be sure to include a color reference. It's difficult to represent colors in an image viewed on a computer screen but by including a common object in the photo that has a similar color, you can give viewers a good idea of the color of your item.

h. Clean and uncluttered background

The focus of your bidder's attention should always be on the item you're selling. Make sure there are no other distractions in your product shot. The best solution is to use a white sheet or tablecloth to create a clean background. If the item you're selling is white or light colored, use a plain dark background. This photography technique is called simplicity. It's easy to achieve simplicity in your photos if you're using the macro setting on your camera; macro shots always have a blurry background so your item stands out.

i. Crop images

When you crop an image, you draw attention to the subject of the photo. Cropping means cutting the image down to size. Cropping is way to get rid of background clutter. Most digital cameras come with free photo editing software that will enable you to crop your images.

j. Take photos while you write

If you photograph your products as you write your descriptions, you'll find it easier to make your images consistent with your description. As you write your description, handling the item will help you to find words to describe it.

A clear, crisp image is the most essential element of your product shots, using out-of-focus shots is the most common mistake sellers make when adding product images. Buyers want to see exactly what they're getting, and a blurry picture makes that impossible. Use a tripod to hold your camera steady and take more than one photo.

B. Free and low-cost photo software

With photo editing software, you can put finishing touches on your images. If you're going to use software to edit your photos, you need to make sure that your changes don't alter the color of your item. Someone who bid on a sky blue dress is going to be annoyed if they receive a gray one. Of course, you should never use software to digitally remove blemishes on your item. That is dishonest, and will anger buyers who purchase something that doesn't look near as good in real life as it did in your listing. There are a number of places where you can find free or cheap image software -

- eBay Picture Services - You can crop, rotate, brighten, or change the contrast in your images and drop the results straight into your listings.
- Your digital camera's software - Most digital camera brands come with their own image editing software.
- Irfanview Software - It's easy to use and has all the tools you need to make quality images. You can also bulk edit your images.

- Gnu Image Manipulation Program – This is an open-source community's answer to Adobe Photoshop. The software is free for you to download and use but it's as complex as Photoshop so it's very easy to get lost in all the possibilities.
- Adobe Photoshop Elements - This software is Adobe's low-cost alternative to Photoshop, it is $139.99 as compared to Photoshop's $699. Included with the software is membership to photoshop.com. This is a great resource for people who have outgrown free software but who don't need a full professional suite of tools.

You can also give your item descriptions a professional look by adding a theme. It's like the frame on a picture. It draws the viewer in and gives an idea of what the listing is about. Auctiva's auction management program is $9.95 per month and offers a range of templates you can apply to your listings and they include your own images. They also have a free option but if you are serious about eBay and making your listings professional it is worth the $9.95 a month.

2. The Right Category

A. <u>Choosing a category</u>

When you start listing an auction on eBay, one of the first things you have to do is select the category and subcategories for your item. By following a few simple tips about category selection you'll attract more targeted bidders to your auction listings and ensure that your listing isn't penalized in Best Match.

a. Let eBay help find what buyers are looking for

Even if you're sure what category you think is the best one for your item, it's always worthwhile to double-check and see where buyers are looking for similar items. Go to the Sell Your Item page and type the keywords for your item in the search field. Use words you think a buyer would use to describe your item. eBay will then give you a breakdown of the different categories that kind of item has been recently listed under. You'll also see what percentage of the item is listed in each category suggestion. These results give you useful information -

- Categories where similar items are most commonly found
- Categories you might not have considered
- An indication that you might consider listing in two categories
- Categories that won't give you high results
- Some surprising categories

By listing in two categories, you can double your items exposure to buyers who browse by category. The benefit of doing this will outweigh the cost of paying for a second category, it doubles your insertion fee and any listing upgrades.

b. Use a keyword search

The Select a Category search will give you a list of common categories and sub-categories, doing a keyword search from eBay will give you the number of items in each category that day. To do this, enter the words in the search box and click Search. It's a good idea to check the completed and current listings in a keyword search, then adjust your category choices according to the results you get.

c. Look at your competition

If the category or sub-category for your item is swamped with your competitor's products, you might want to think about shifting your products to a related but different, category to get them more exposure. The amount of competition you have is only one consideration. The quality of competition is something else you should keep tabs on. If your competitors in a category have higher Feedback, a stronger sales history, cheaper shipping, better images, or more attractive terms of service than you do, you might want to think about moving your items into a category that does not compete directly with them.

Sometimes an item just doesn't sell. If it's an item that's sold well in the past, it might be nothing more than a bad day. More often than not, items don't sell because they don't get in front of enough potential buyers. Changing categories can fix this problem. Items that don't sell are simple to relist it's a couple of clicks. But this time, try listing it in one of the categories you discovered through your research.

B. <u>Avoid the wrong category</u>

New sellers choose the wrong category for their items. It happens a lot more often than you'd think. It happens when sellers are creating several listings at once or they're using an old template that already has a category selected. Another common mistake sellers make is not paying for placement in more than one category when the item they're selling would benefit from the exposure.

Beware of trying to get more attention for your items by placing them in a whole bunch of random categories. You are breaking the terms of the User Agreement you have with eBay by placing items in misleading categories. eBay can cancel your auction if you misuse the category labels. Putting your auctions in the wrong categories does nothing to make your item more visible to your targeted buyers. If you have the option of a category connected to a specific keyword, you should choose that over listing your item in the generic Other category.

Persistent buyers might be able to find you, but window shoppers, impulse buyers, and the bulk of eBay's traffic will be more attracted to keyword-specific categories, brand names, and styles. eBay keeps a close eye on categories, and reorganizes them frequently based on patterns and traffic numbers. When they notice items being sold under "Other" they try to find or create a category that fits it. It's easy to imagine a buyer looking for your specific item but that's not always the way it works. You need to imagine a buyer looking for something, and then finding your item and realizing that it's what they were looking for all along.

If your item doesn't have much competition and doesn't seem to have its own category, there's no reason you can't try listing it in several categories. Listing your item in the wrong category is, against eBay policy, but unique items may require some testing before they find a home. The first seller to find a category it sells in will reap rewards.

It's been said that you can sell anything on eBay except soup. That may be true, but soup sales are also banned by eBay policy. There are dozens of categories that are either prohibited or only allowed under certain conditions. Perishable goods like soup are a no-no, as are items that are illegal, hazardous, or copyright infringements. Buyers and sellers have learned the hard way, and eBay has banned just about anything that has caused them legal problems in the past. Before you put up anything double-check the prohibited and restricted items page.

3. Auction Title

A. __The right keywords__

Your auction title is the first impression visitors get of your auction and it can make it or break it. There are two main reasons your title is important -

- Good keywords attract search traffic on eBay
- Well-written titles catch the eye of buyers and make you stand out

You might have the best item in the world but if your buyers can't find your listing, you won't make a sale. Keywords are words or phrases that describe or name your item. They're the words people type into the eBay search box when looking for an item. That means the keywords you use in your title are the most important words in your entire auction. Use the wrong words and chances of people finding your auction decrease. Now that keyword relevance plays a role in where your listings show up in the search results, it's more important to make sure you've got them right.

To find the right words for your title, you have to think like a buyer. What words would a buyer use to search for products like yours? The more accurately your keywords describe what you sell, the more likely your buyers are to click on it. You can also do a search for items you're thinking of selling and pay attention to the listings that are making it to the top. Always include the brand name of your items in your auction titles. If your target market is likely to search for the model number of your product, include that too. Another thing to do is stuff your title with information. Your title doesn't need to flow like a perfect sentence. It should be a list of searchable keywords.

Now that you know how important it is to have a keyword-rich listing title. You should use research tools to discover what potential buyers are typing into search boxes. Here are a few tools to use to find keywords -

- Terapeak - Find closed listings that had your keywords in their titles, filter out the keywords you don't want to include, then check the success rate of the remaining keywords.
- eBay's Completed Listings - Search for items similar to yours. Sort completed listings by the highest price and take a close look at the titles of items that attract the most bidders and the highest final selling values.
- eBay Pulse - Get a list of eBay's top 10 search words. The category and subcategory keywords will be more useful than the overall top 10. Use the drop-down menu to select your category and subcategories, notice how the list of largest eBay Stores changes each time you select a new category.

- eBay Estimator - The eBay Estimator tool shows you which keywords and categories are most popular so you can add them to your listing titles. Once you learn how to make the most of this tool it can help you if you're stuck in keyword limbo.
- Search Google - By searching the web with you'll see what keywords other people use to describe your items.
- Keyword suggestion tools - Google AdWords Keyword Tool and Keyword Discovery's Search Term Suggestion Tool. These free keyword suggestion tools measure the number of times Internet users type different keywords into the major search engines.

One advantage to using these tools is that you can increase your chances of showing up off eBay. Some people start their eBay purchase cycle with Google.

B. Get the most out of your title

Fifty – five characters is all the space you have in your title, so every one of those characters should count. If you waste some of your characters on non-essential or distracting words, you are not writing a great title. Every single character has one purpose, to draw targeted traffic to your listing. It used to be commonplace on eBay for sellers to use gimmicks to catch buyers' eyes. Problem is, no one searches them and they make your listing look amateurish, it also reduces the chance of being found.

Not every product goes by one common name, so it's important to consider multiple wordings and spellings your potential buyers may use. For common products, eBay will show results for all the variations. For less-popular products you'll need to think about the different terms people might use to search for your item.

a. Common misspellings

Everyone makes spelling mistakes and eBay buyers are no different. If your product name has a common misspelling, put that in your title if you have space. Don't worry that people will think that you can't spell. Fatfingers.com is a great resource for finding common misspellings.

b. Two-word/one-word combinations

Another common spelling variation is words that can be split in two. If you have space, use these common variations in your title.

c. Multiple number variations

Keep in mind number variations, Software, movie titles, video games, musical recordings, and many other products have numbers that indicate the version or the series. Your buyers are using both the numerals and words to search for the items, so your title should try to include those possibilities.

d. Use singular, not plural

You should always use the singular form of an item in your listing title. If someone searches for something they will get results that include the plural form. That means you're pretty much guaranteed to get more visitors if you leave the "s" off the end. Be aware that potential customers might not click your listing because of poor grammar. The key is to find the right balance so a title will make your listing show up in their search results and encourage viewers to click through.

e. Punctuation

Something else to consider is your use of punctuation in titles. If you write a dress size as 10/12, your item will show up in both searches for size 10 and 12. This is because eBay's search engine treats slashes, commas, and hyphens as spaces. Avoid using tildes (~). If you write that dress size as 10~12, your item will show up in neither sizes. eBay's search engine don't treat tildes as spaces, instead of saying the dress is around size 10 or 12, you are saying that the dress is "10~12".

C. eBay shorthand

You've probably noticed some eBay titles look like secret code. They use "words" (always in capital letters) like COA, NIB, NOS, and so on. These are acronyms for commonly used terms and experienced sellers find them very useful because they don't take up much space in the title. Acronyms can save you characters for keywords that can't be shortened easily. There are 27 characters in the phrase "Certificate of Authenticity", an experienced sellerr would use the acronym COA, which frees up characters.

When using acronyms, remember typical eBay buyers don't use acronyms as search terms. Don't count on the acronyms themselves to give you visibility in search results, count on them to draw your buyers' eyes when they are scanning a list of similar items. If these acronyms get your buyer to click through to your description, then they have accomplished their main purpose. eBay provides a list of many of the acronyms sellers use. Here is a list of the most commonly used ones -

A/O	all original	MOC	mint on card
BIN	Buy It Now	MWBT	mint with both tags
BNWT	brand new with tags	MWMT	mint with mint tags
CC	credit card	NBW	never been worn
DUP	duplicate	NIB	new in box
EX/MT	excellent to mint condition	NOS	new old stock
F and FN	fine condition (used)	NR	no reserve
FORG	forgery	NRFB	never removed from box
FPFH or PFH	from pet-free home		
FS	factory-sealed	NW	never worn
FSFH or SFH	from smoke-free home	NWOT	new without tags
G or GD	good condition (used)	NWT	new with tags
HTF	hard to find	OB	original box
LE	limited edition	OOAK	one of a kind
LTD	limited	OOP	out of print
MIB	mint in box	P	poor condition (used)
MIMB	mint in mint box	PP	PayPal
MIP	mint in package	RI	reissue
MIMP	mint in mint package	S&H, S/H, or SH	shipping and handling
MIOP	mint in opened package		
MNB	mint condition no box	SCR	scratch
		SZ	size
		TOS	terms of sale

Occasionally, you'll notice acronyms that aren't on eBay's list. Sellers in very specialized markets develop a kind of shorthand jargon that is meaningful within their niche. Since the use of acronyms is related to the thing being sold, it takes a bit of experience to tell exactly which ones you have to know. Whatever acronyms you use, be sure to write them out in full in your item description so there's no mystery for your buyer.

D. Formatting

It's not enough to use searchable keywords; you have to think about how your title looks, and how people will read it. Here are strategies that will help -

a. Put keywords in key places

You have to be smart about where in your title you place each word. It's easier for eBay's search engine to find the information at the beginning of your title than the information at the end and that means you'll do better in the Best Match search with your best keywords at the start.

b. DON'T USE ALL CAPS

When writing your listing title, DON'T USE ALL CAPS. Titles containing all capital letters are hard to read, and online conversation treats all-caps like yelling, which annoys people. You should capitalize the first letter of each word in your title, titles written in all lower case will blend into the search list, making them harder to see.

c. Bonus

Offering a free bonus that you'll send to the winning bidder is a great way to entice more viewers to click through from your title to your listing. If you're offering a bonus, add the term "+ bonus" or "free bonus" to your listing as an incentive for people to click through.

The best way to find out which titles work best is to test different ones and track the results of each.

4. Auction Salescopy

A. **Writing salescopy**

Salescopy is writing that sells and few sellers know how to put the secrets of salescopy to work in their auction listings.   Creating product descriptions that really sell your items is one of the most important skills you can learn if you're serious about making money on eBay. You'd be surprised how many people don't pay enough attention to this element of an eBay auction.   Many eBay sellers just copy and paste descriptive product copy they found on a manufacturer's website into their listing or stick in a few bullet points and a paragraph about payments or shipping.

DON'T' DO THAT! If you put a little effort into making your product descriptions work harder and try to make your auctions stand out from the crowd, you're going to gain an advantage over your competition. You'are also likely to attract higher bids. It's not hard to write descriptions that grab and hold a reader attention and get them to bid. There are two reasons this works so well -

- Good salescopy gives readers everything they need to see the value of your products for themselves. Once they start to see the value, they start to get excited about the possibility of owning it themselves. It answers the question, "What's in it for ME?"
- Salescopy guides your reader through the stages of the sales process

A well-written salesletter carefully arranged in a series of steps can generate excitement, address possible objections, and reassure the visitor that they'll be making a great purchase. Long copy allows you to guide your reader toward the buying decision with the finesse of an experienced salesperson. Writing successful long copy is a learned skill. You won't be able to write a great long copy the first time. Remember this writing salescopy is not an art it is science. That means it's a skill that anyone can learn. You don't need years of practice or be a gifted writer.

If you can follow this formula and implement all of the elements required you can have strong, effective copy on your listing, no matter what your grammar skills are. If you're worried that you're not a professional writer, or that you don't sound like a salesperson when you write, that's okay. A little personality goes a long way in salescopy. Your visitors don't want to be dragged through a sales pitch, they want to buy products from somebody they can relate to. Before you open a new listing and start writing, it's important that you do some research to learn more about the customers you'll be writing to. Understanding your target audience and finding out how your competitors are selling their items are the two areas to focus on in your research.

a. Know your competition

Search for completed listings of the same items you're going to sell, and check out a few of your competitors in the results pages. You should be on the lookout for -

- The auctions with the highest selling price and most bids and see how their Salescopy encouraged bidding
- The auctions with the lowest number of bids and lowest selling price to how their Salescopy might have discouraged bidding
- Auctions with a lot of bids but a lower selling price than other similar auctions to see if there was anything in the salescopy could have reduced the value of the item

By digging into the salescopy for similar items that sold for the highest and lowest prices, you will get some ideas for selling your item effectively, as well as insight into what doesn't work.

b. Know your buyers

If you know your buyers and how they behave on eBay, you'll find it much easier to write a description that gives them all the information and incentive they need to make an informed decision on whether or not to bid on your item. If you understand their motivations, you'll also be able to relate to them on an emotional level, meaning you'll have a good idea of what to say and how to say it in your product descriptions. The first thing to understand about people who buy on eBay is there are a few common traits that make it possible to separate your audience of eBay buyers into six groups you need to appeal to -

- The know-it-all - an expert on the item you're selling or in the related subject area. They will look for specific things to convince themselves of your item's value. They may ask you specific questions and because they're likely to have a good idea of the true value of your item, they won't be pushed into bidding by salescopy.
- The serious buyer - looking for exactly what you have to sell and may have searched for the exact model number or brand that you're offering. They already have done their research and made their decision to buy. It's up to you to convince them that your item fits their needs and will meet their expectations.
- The researcher - leaves no stone unturned before buying an item. They're wary about buying online but know that there are bargains to be had. You need to answer every question or concern they might have about your item and provide them with links to web pages where they can verify your information, helping you earn their trust.
- The impulse buyer – usually is just be browsing with no real intention to

buy, but they found your auction and they're interested and open to bid. Your description has to convince them that they need what you have to offer and that this opportunity is too good to pass up. Your description needs to compel them to place a bid immediately to try their luck or make an instant purchase using Buy It Now.

- The bargain hunter - The better the item appears in your description, and the lower your starting price, the more likely it is that they will bid on your item. They're the ones who start bidding frenzies by bidding early in the hope of snagging a bargain.
- The newbie - fairly new to eBay or possibly even the Internet in general and like the researcher, may be skeptical about buying online. Worried about being scammed, they need to be reassured that you're an honest seller with a good reputation. They want to know how they will pay for the item, how it will be shipped, and that they can contact you with any questions.

Not everyone is going to fall into these categories but you will find that most do. If you can answer all their questions, worries, and concerns in your listing, then you're likely to attract more bids. Knowing your audience as well as possible also helps you build a loyal group of customers who will add you to their "Favorite Sellers" list and keep an eye out for your auctions. That means the next time you set up an auction, you'll have a ready-made audience.

B. The steps to great salescopy

Your product description will be the most powerful selling tool you have at your disposal but only if you stop thinking of it just as a description of what you have to sell. It's an entire sales process and it's time to jump in.

a. Position your item as unique

Offering something unique is vital on eBay, there are so many auctions competing for the attention of bidders. Highlighting your item's unique selling points, the benefits of your item that make it unique in the eyes of your customers, will make it more desirable to them. It'll also set it apart from your competitors' auctions. Other ways to make your item appear unique include -

- Creating more value
- Adding value by offering free bonuses
- Bundling your item

The key is to find one thing that your competition doesn't offer, and then use it as the foundation of your product description. Unique features make up what's called a unique selling proposition or USP. This can be something you discovered while using the item or it could be something you find out by researching the item online. Make sure you emphasize it and the benefits that come from it.

b. Headline and sub-headline

Each eBay listing includes a title, possibly a subtitle, which appears in search results and in other locations on eBay. This keyword-rich description of your product is designed to attract potential bidders and get them to view your listing. Once visitors have clicked this title, they'll see the most important elements on your listing page directly below it - your headline and sub-headline. The most important attention-grabbing tool is your headline. It's the first thing potential bidders see and just like the neon sign outside the movie theater. A great headline and sub-headline should -

- Create a problem that the reader can identify with
- Stress the main benefit of your product in solving that problem
- Generate excitement and a desire in your readers to find out more
- Include main keywords to make sure your listing rises to the top of searches

To get your visitors excited and draw them into your salesletter, your headline should be packed with benefits that are sure to appeal to your target audience and have them scrambling to find out more. Your sub-headline should build on the benefits shared in the headline by showing bidders how they'll benefit.

c. Create the problem

Once you have grabbed your visitors' attention with your headline and sub-headline, appeal to them by describing the problem they're facing in more detail. This will show them that you understand the problems they're facing and it puts you in the perfect position to offer your product as the solution to their problem later. At this point your reader should be nodding in agreement. You can do this with any product, simply by thinking about the problems that would compel someone to go out and look for a solution.

d. Identify with the reader

Before you can convince readers that you have a solution to their problem, you need to convince them that you truly understand their problem, and that you can relate to them. This is an approach that a professional salesperson will take when talking with you in a retail store, and it's just as effective and necessary in your salescopy.

e. Tell a story

eBay is different from many other commercial websites because you're an individual dealing with individuals. It's a good idea to write a little story around the item you're selling. Not only does this add some life to the auction, but if the item happens to have an interesting background, that in itself becomes a selling point. People like to show off things they've just bought and if there's a story to go with it that they can tell their friends. Tell a story that will bring a smile to your reader's face.

f. Overview of your solution

Now that your readers are enjoying themselves and reading your story, you're ready to expand upon the promise of the resolution that you have been building up to. You don't have to explain how it works yet, share an easy-to-read overview of how your product can make their lives better. Let readers see the value of what you're offering and show them that it's a great solution to the problem you introduced.

g. Describe your item in detail

When it comes to describing your item, don't leave anything out. Remember the aim of your description is to answer every possible question potential bidders have. Include all details about your item like -

- Brand
- Make and model
- Condition
- Warranty
- Packaging details
- Any other relevant information

Other details you should include are descriptions of any interesting features, things that make it stand out from other similar items. All these details help convince bidders of the item's value. Always include images along with your description. More expensive items need more images to sell them because it's a bigger risk for someone to buy something expensive without seeing it. When you're sharing product details with your reader, it's also a good idea to include your email address and invite people to email you with questions. This is a good way to start building relationships and establishing your credibility.

h. Features and benefits

After describing the features of your product in detail, you should think of as many ways as possible to translate those features into benefits. A feature is an attribute of a product. A benefit is a way that a product solves a problem for its owner. The benefits stress what your product can do for buyers and how it can solve their problems.

i. Establish credibility

Throughout your product description you should always take advantage of opportunities to build your credibility in the eyes of bidders. Establishing your credibility helps your readers feel safe enough to buy from you. You need to reassure them that you have all the right experience to be the person they should buy from, and that you are trustworthy and honest. There are many ways to do this -

- Position yourself as an expert
- Be honest when describing your items
- Use testimonials from people who have bought your products
- Use proper spelling and grammar

Often just being honest and upfront about what you're selling and including a link to your feedback is enough to convince bidders of your credibility.

j. Bonuses

At this point, your readers are convinced of the value of your product or service. They want what you have to offer and they should trust you enough to want it from you. But they may still be a little reluctant to commit by bidding on your listing. One way to help potential bidders overcome their hesitation is by offering one or more bonus items that you'll throw in free with their purchase. Obviously, you're not going to include bonuses with everything you list on eBay but if you're listing an auction where the winning bidder will receive a package of multiple items, or a higher-value item, throwing in a few bonuses can be a great way to get people excited about placing a bid. The more bonuses you offer, the higher the perceived value of your fixed price listing or auction will be to your audience. Bonuses don't have to be expensive, remember their sole purpose is to increase the perceived value of your listing.

k. Terms and conditions

One of the most common causes of disputes, withdrawn bids, and misunderstandings on eBay is sellers failing to make their terms and conditions clear. When you list your auction, don't rely on bidders to click away from your listing to read about your shipping, payment details and return policy. Include these details in your item description so bidders know what's involved in buying from you. Be sure to include -

- Payment options
- Bidding and/or shipping restrictions
- Shipping and handling fees
- Taxes and duty
- Warranty and refund policy
- Feedback guidelines
- Contact information
- Delivery details

At the end of this section, provide your email address again, saying, "Please email me with any questions about shipping and payment options. I'm happy to answer all questions and will get back to you as soon as I can!"

l. A strong guarantee

Adding a money-back guarantee is another proven marketing technique that is an excellent way to increase sales. Saying "We stand by our products. If you aren't satisfied with your purchase, send it back for a full refund" reassures bidders and shows that you have complete confidence in your items for sale. It also separates you from your competitors who don't offer a guarantee. You may be tempted to put a time limit on the guarantee, but a 30-day, or even 90-day, money-back guarantee doesn't carry much weight. Guarantees that don't state a time limit outperform those that do because they convey a much stronger message that encourages more bids and purchases.

You may get a few returns but most people don't return items unless they genuinely have a serious complaint with it, in which case it's only right that they get a refund. Any returns you do get are outweighed by the extra sales you generate through your guarantee.

m. Create urgency

To persuade someone to take action, it's important to create a sense of urgency. People tend to put things off when they think they can come back and do it later, so you need to tell them why it's important for them to act now, rather than later. Auctions are urgent by their nature but it's still a good idea to instill a sense of urgency into your salescopy to encourage viewers to take action.

n. Ask for the sale

With your salescopy written, your guarantee in place, and your bonus offers on the table, your reader is no longer nervous about placing a bid, making the purchase, or outbidding the next potential buyer. This is the point in your sales process where many eBayers drop the ball. Now that you've convinced viewers that they want your item you need to ask for the sale. Without including a call to action you're stuck hoping that potential bidders will know what to do when they hit the end of your salescopy. Your call to action doesn't need to be long; it needs to be clear. A great way to lead into this is by restating the main benefits of your product, then asking people to place a bid.

o. The P.S.

The P.S. is the second most important element in your listing, after the headline. That's because most people won't take the time to read every word in your listing. Instead, they'll skim over it, taking note of a few key points that interest them, until they reach the end of your listing. At this point, they'll be looking at your call to action and making a decision about whether to place a bid or not. Including an exciting P.S. at the end of your listing, gives your auction one last chance to grab your visitors' attention and get them to bid. Make sure it's packed with benefits, urgency, and a final call to action.

Yes this formula is time-consuming at first and if you're selling low-value items, it's probably overkill. For higher-value items, this formula simply can't be beat for getting visitors excited about your listing and getting them to take action.

C. <u>Enjoyable to read salescopy</u>

Make sure the formatting of your listing in attractive and appealing so that it looks professional and easy to read. eBay's Sell Your Item form makes it easy to do this. After you create your listing title and choose your category or categories, you'll be taken to a page where you can add product information and images, then format your listing using a full-featured HTML editor. Here are a few things you can do -

- Use eBay's suggestions to choose one or more categories
- Enable product details
- Edit your title and subtitle
- Add pictures and a Gallery picture
- Use eBay's Listing Designer to add a template
- Add a visitor counter
- Specify delivery details with eBay's Shipping Wizard

When it comes to formatting the salescopy you write for your listing, eBay's What You See Is What You Get HTML editor makes it a breeze to create a crisp, attractive listing that's sure to appeal to potential buyers. If you go overboard with crazy colors, fonts, and images, it's just as easy to create an ugly, tacky listing that's impossible to read. Here are some formatting tips -

- Use dark text on a light background
- Grab attention with a large, colorful headline
- Use a plain, legible font, align your text to the left and don't go crazy with color
- Emphasize important information with bolding and italics
- Break up longer passages of text with subheads
- Set key points and features in bullet points
- Check your spelling

By following this formula you'll be able to create product descriptions that engage visitors to your auctions and make your listings stand out from the crowd. Remember, this formula incorporates tested online selling techniques that have been proven time and time again to create excitement and make sales. Don't forget to use your auction description to spell out exactly what your buyers can expect, when they can expect it, and how much they'll pay for it so you can protect your seller rating.

5. Set Up Your Auction

A. <u>Evaluate your listing</u>

When creating a listing, there is a variety of options that can appear intimidating if you don't know what you're doing. The biggest mistake eBay newbies make when creating their listing is to become overwhelmed by these options, then just pick strategies at random in the final stages before listing their auction. If you fall into this trap, you can end up paying for extra features that don't generate extra income. To maximize your chances of creating a profitable listing every time, you need to be able to look at every element of that listing and know the answer to this question - "Do I know that this element measurably increases the profit I am likely to earn?" If the answer is yes, good. If the answer is no keep reading. When setting up your auctions, one of your first decisions is which selling format to use.

a. Auction-style listings

The Auction-style format is eBay's most popular. An item is listed and interested viewers outbid one another to win the item. The one downside, for both buyers and sellers, is that you have to wait for the auction to run its course to complete the sale. If you're running standard auctions, you'll be turning over your inventory slowly and one of the keys to success on eBay is fast turnover of stock. To solve this problem and add some variety. You can choose to list your auctions for one, three, five, seven, or even 10 days. Although longer auctions are more common on eBay, each listing duration has certain benefits. Think about these factors when choosing a listing duration -

- Your buyers
- Time limitations
- Your selling volume

In addition, you'll want to look at the advantages and disadvantages of each -

- One day – These are the shortest auctions available. If you're selling time-sensitive items, you might need to use a one-day listing. High-volume sellers listing a lot of identical items are the main users of one-day auctions. They can list an unlimited number of identical items simultaneously. To be eligible to post one-day listings you need a PayPal account and a minimum Feedback score of five or without PayPal, 10 positive Feedback.
- Three Days - Three-day listings allow for quick turnaround but with slightly more time to get your item in front of interested buyers. If you've tested your market and discovered that most of your target audience shops on the weekend, you don't have to waste money listing on unproductive days.
- Five days - This means quicker turnaround, but with longer durations so

more viewers see your item, it's all about finding the right balance for you. Another advantage of three and five-day listings is that they allow you more flexibility in timing the end of your auctions without paying extra for the scheduling feature.

- Seven days – This is the standard auction format and recommended for all new sellers. Having your item posted for a full week allows time for buyers to find your item, while still giving your listing a reasonably short window of availability. Seven-day auctions are the most successful format, in terms of sell-through rates and highest average sales price.
- Ten days - For rare or unique items that don't have mass-market appeal, a 10-day listing can give you more exposure. If you're not in a rush to sell your item, a longer listing time can increase the chances of making a successful sale. However, 10-day listings are a paid upgrade and will cost you an extra .40.

Online Auction listings have other options you can explore -

a. Reserve Price

For sellers who want to list their item in an auction format and ensure they get a minimum price, eBay offers the Reserve Price. A reserve price is the lowest price you're willing to sell the item for. Reserve prices are kept secret for the duration of the auction and if none of the bids you receive are high enough to meet the reserve price, you don't have to sell your item.

b. Buy It Now

In most categories, when you choose the Buy It Now option in with an Online Auction listing, your item can sell two ways -

- A buyer purchases your item at the BIN price and the auction ends immediately.
- Someone bids on your item, which eliminates the BIN option, and the auction proceeds normally.

For some categories the option to Buy It Now remains available until the bid price reaches 50% of the BIN price. There are two strategies that work well for using Buy It Now with a regular auction -

- Perceived value stimulates early bidding by making initial bidders feel like they're getting a great deal.
- Instant gratification, on the other hand, is a way for you to take a shot at an instant sale at a fixed price.

A great time to use BIN pricing is around the holidays, when people are shopping for gifts, they're often in a hurry and don't have the time to wait for the end of an auction. In these instances, bidders will often pay a premium to get the item sooner rather than later.

b. Fixed Price Listings

Fixed Price listings aren't auctions. When you put an item up for sale, you set a price and shoppers either buy your item at that price or it doesn't sell. It can be used for one or more items and it will continue until time runs out or all your items are sold. To list in this format, you have to sell the item for at least $1.00 and you'll also need to maintain a minimum Feedback score of 5 if you have a PayPal account and accept PayPal as a payment method. If you're selling through a Premium or Anchor store, you'll have to be PayPal Verified. If you don't have a PayPal account, you'll need a minimum of 10 Feedback. If the Feedback requirements are preventing you from using Fixed Price, you can become ID Verified and get around the Feedback problem that way.

Top sellers on eBay often use the Fixed Price format for new merchandise. They usually have a steady supply of inventory, know the retail value of the item, and have a clear idea of their profit margin and what buyers are willing to pay

a. Buy It Now

You can cater to your more impatient buyers, and make sales faster, by eliminating the auction altogether and listing your items as Buy It Now. Whatever price you set is the price they sell for.

b. Best Offer

This is a free feature that allows you to accept offers on the item before the bidding ends. This feature lets buyers click a button in your listing and send you a message explaining their offer, to buy three for the price of two, haggle you down a couple of dollars, or just beg for a discount. Whatever the offer, the option is free and it's easy to accept or decline offers. You can set a range of prices that you will accept and when you receive an offer within that range, your offer will be accepted automatically. The easiest place to review these offers is through your My eBay page.

Best Offers can increase the time spent administering your auctions but they can help you turn over inventory faster, eliminating the need to relist the item if you just want to get rid of it. This feature works best for multiple-item listings, as buyers can make offers to buy in bulk.

c. Store Listings

eBay Stores are specialty sites where sellers can display all their listings exclusively and tell buyers about their business through their own eBay storefront. If you create your own eBay Store, you'll be able to list items in Store Inventory format. These are different from regular auctions -

- Items are listed at a set price
- Initial listing fees are lower but final value fees are higher
- Subtitle is cheaper to use, and listing upgrades last 30 days
- Store listings can have an unlimited duration
- You can add Best Offer

Once you get your feet wet and start developing a serious eBay business, opening your own store is a great next step. You'll get lots of opportunities to cut your fees and boost your profit margin, provided you understand a bit about what types of listing work best for different products. Setting up an eBay Store costs $15.95 per month for a basic store and requires a PayPal account with a credit card on file or a minimum feedback score of 20.

d. Classified Ad Listings

eBay knows that not everything can reasonably be sold as an auction, some things just need more communication than a Best Offer negotiation. If you sell a product or service that requires a lot of back-and-forth with a prospective buyer, you might want to check out eBay Classified Ads. Classified Ads are listings that give information about a product or service in order to generate leads. They aren't part of the auction process at all, so bids can't be placed on them. Any sales made as a result of your listing have to take place outside eBay.

eBay doesn't want to divert traffic or sales from their regular auction listings, but they do want to attract sellers who might not otherwise use eBay to sell their wares. So Classified Ads are available as 30-day listings only for certain subcategories within these categories -

- Businesses for Sale
- Trade Show Displays
- Real Estate
- Specialty Services
- Travel
- "Everything Else"

Ads are $9.95 for 30 days and your ad shows up with all the other auctions in the category you selected, but your listing will say Classified Ad where your bid price would normally be. Interested buyers will contact you with the contact information you supplied, which will show up at the top of your listing.

B. <u>Listing upgrades</u>

eBay fees are broken down into small charges that don't look like much by themselves, but once added together, can total a lot of cash. Some of these fees are unavoidable and charged on all auctions. There are some insertion fees you can control by limiting the number of listing upgrades you choose to use. The important thing to remember is that every upgrade you decide to include in your listing is costing you money and potentially lowering your profit margin on each sale. There's only one way to know which listing options perform and which don't, and that is research. These are the most common eBay listing upgrades.

a. Gallery picture

A Gallery photo is a small thumbnail image that's displayed on the eBay search results page. It's an effective option that used to cost money, but is now free. With a Gallery photo, potential customers can see what your product looks like as soon as they get their search results. Plus, many shoppers like to use the Gallery View for browsing eBay, which means that products without a Gallery picture won't show up. Most sellers will take advantage of the Gallery photo feature, you might want to consider paying for a Gallery Plus upgrade. Gallery Plus adds an "Enlarge" icon below your Gallery image on search results pages. A buyer can click or hover over the icon to see a larger version of the picture.

Gallery Plus is beneficial if you're selling an item that is visually appealing. Because it partially obscures nearby listings, it's a good way to make sure your item photo can't be missed. If you host your photos through eBay's Picture Services, Gallery Plus will also allow your potential bidders to view all your listing photos from the search results. The fee for Gallery Plus photos is 35 cents for listings 10 days and under, or $1 for 30 days even if you host your own photos.

b. Bolding

Putting your item's title in bold print for $2 (for listings under 10 days) or $4 (for 30-day listings) makes your title stand out from the many others out there. If you expect your item to sell for more than $25, the cost for a bold-titled listing might be worthwhile as long as it attracts more bidders and increases your profits, rather than cutting into them.

c. Subtitle

You can add a subtitle to your listing title with some descriptive information to entice bidders to click through to your auction. Keywords in your subtitle will not show up in a basic search, their sole purpose is to persuade searchers to click through to your listings. We recommend the Subtitle option. It breaks up the repetitive pattern of the search results and makes people stop and look. It also gives you the opportunity to add details that shoppers are looking for. It costs 50 cents for 10 days, and $1.50 for 30 days.

d. Value Pack

The Value Pack gives you a Gallery Plus picture, a Subtitle, and Listing Designer for only 65 cents for 10 days (and under), and $2 for 30 days. This is a great option to use if you have the sort of listing that needs a big boost.

There are a lot of other options for listing upgrades available, from 10-cent Listing Designer templates right up to a Home Page featured listing. We cannot stress enough how important it is for you to consider all eBay's fees when deciding which listing upgrades to choose for your auctions. It doesn't take much for these fees to get out of control and you may end up handing over all your profits to eBay. Do your research and use the eBay and PayPal Fee Calculator to run a few scenarios.

C. Pricing strategies

For any eBay seller, newbie or professional, one of the biggest questions is What's a good starting price for my auction?

a. Starting bid

Setting a starting bid for your eBay auctions can be difficult and there is no one correct answer for any product or seller. Where you decide to start your bidding depends on the amount of risk you are willing to take. The best way to get an idea of where to start your bidding is by researching completed listings for items similar to yours. By looking at the final prices other sellers have reached, then comparing those with their starting bids, you'll be able to see what strategies work for different types of products. Many eBay sellers will tell you that by starting the bidding at 99 cents, they can create bidding and sell the item for more than they could have if they started the bidding at a higher price. An advantage of starting your bidding low is that when a potential bidder sorts their search results in order of lowest prices first, your item will appear near the top.

You need to be cautious when setting a low initial bid. If you're not very certain your item will sell, you may want to start the bidding for the lowest price you're willing to take for it. This way, you don't put yourself in the position of having to take a loss on an item that you could relist at a later date. While starting your bidding at a higher price will protect you from selling your item at a loss, it's likely this tactic will turn away some bidders who don't think they are getting a very good deal.

b. Reserve price

Another option for protecting your bottom line is to use a reserve price. This is a price below which you will not sell an item. You specify the reserve price when creating your listing, but it is not visible to bidders during the auction. As the bids come in, the listing will display "Reserve not met" beside the current bid until the reserve price is met. After that, the message changes to "Reserve met" and bidders can then win the auction. In addition to protecting you from taking a loss, reserve prices let you keep your initial listing fees in check by allowing you to start the bidding low. Keep in mind that reserve price auctions are subject to a fee. Even if your item does not sell, eBay keeps the reserve fee. Fees for adding a reserve to your auction are $2 for items priced below $200 and 1% of the reserve price for items worth over $200. You should use high starting bids or a reserve price only for items that have a very small market or are very expensive.

Most eBay sellers find that a low start price is the best way to get people bidding and drive the final sale price of your item up. If you're willing to risk it this approach can bring in the greatest returns.

D. <u>Timing your auctions</u>

Most auctions see a flurry of bids in the final minutes. That's because people who have been watching the item throughout the listing time are finally getting involved. They don't place bids earlier because they don't want to drive up the price of the item. Since eBay introduced Best Match as its default sort method, your listing won't automatically get prime billing at the end of your auction listing. It's still worth paying attention to timing because people can still sort search results by "time ending soonest". As long as your DSRs and keywords are on par with your competition, strategically timing your auctions can still give you an edge.

When do most people visit eBay to check auctions? It depends who you ask and what their target market is. In general, statistics show that traffic on eBay is highest on weekends but the site also buzzes with traffic on weeknights between 5 and 9 when most people get home from work. There are plenty of exceptions to this general trend. With all other listing options, do some research to find out when other sellers in your market are ending their auctions, then follow up by testing a few start and end times. If you're diligent and keep track of the results, you should be able to determine the optimum day and time to end auctions for each specific item you are selling. One thing to remember when determining the start and end times of your auctions is that eBay operates on Pacific Time. If you live on the East Coast and you want your auction to end on a Wednesday night, make sure that you take different time zones into account. eBay posts the eBay official time via a link on the bottom left of every page.

E. Search Visibility Analysis tool

When a customer types keywords into the eBay search box, they'll get back all the listings relevant to their keywords, ranked in order based on "Best Match." Best Match ranks listings based on several different factors, including how well an item matches the search criteria, price, shipping cost, and the seller's performance record. It's not difficult to see where your items rank in the search results, just type different keywords into the search box and see for yourself. That list can't tell you why your items rank where they do. And without knowing why, you can't figure out how to raise your ranking. This is why you need to use the Search Visibility Analysis tool. This can really level the playing field for beginners and it's available to all sellers.

In order to see how one of your listings is doing, enter the item number into the search bar on the Search Visibility Analysis page and run the report. Let's look at all the information you get.

a. Best Match factors

This section shows you how different elements of your listing are affecting your search standing -

- Item and shipping costs
- Free shipping boost
- Sales per impressions
- Seller performance

b. Other factors

- Impressions
- Click-throughs
- Watchers.

~ 70 ~

c. How you rate

You can drill down even deeper by clicking on the "Find Your Listing by Keyword" feature and find out how your listing stacks up against the competition. eBay gives you -

- Price range
- Shipping cost range
- How many others offer free shipping
- Auction versus fixed price
- How many Top-Rated Sellers are you up against
- How many competitors include pre-filled product details

All this data is gold. If you're running multiple listings in the same category, you can check to see how they're all doing by entering the category number in the search bar and run a new report. It gets better, once you've analyzed all your data, eBay gives you tips on what you can do to improve your listing's search ranking and lets you make changes to your listing right on the same page. eBay will walk you through the steps you need to take to get a better ranking, increase your exposure in eBay's search results, and make your listing more appealing to your buyers. The Search Visibility Tool isn't available for all listings. You can check out the exclusions and anything else you need to know on the eBay help page for the Search visibility analysis tool.

6. Payment and Shipping

A. **Payment options**

It's fun to find things to sell, to write up auctions, and to watch the bidding process unfold. At the end of the day, though, it's all about watching the money roll in. You must always receive payment before you ship anything out to your buyers. Many bidders change their minds about their purchase after winning an auction. While eBay enforces laws to protect the seller when this happens, it can be tough to get your money from people who don't pay, and even tougher if you've already sent their item out. Choosing payment strategies is a key part of the eBay sales process. How you ask your customers to pay will affect who bids on your auctions, where they can bid from, how quickly you will receive payment, and how reliable their payments will be. For most categories, sellers need to offer one or more of these electronic payment options -

- PayPal
- ProPay
- Moneybookers
- Paymate
- Credit or Debit card, processed through seller's Internet merchant account.

The most common eBay payment methods are PayPal, credit cards, and escrow services.

a. PayPal

eBay strongly encourages sellers and buyers to use the PayPal system for all their eBay transactions. As part of eBay's recent safe payment policy, sellers with less than 100 Feedback or a dissatisfaction rate of 5% in the last 30 days are required to offer PayPal or a merchant credit card option. Same goes for sellers listing items in higher-risk categories and sub-categories. PayPal is a system that facilitates the transfer of money between buyers and sellers. It allows you to accept credit card payments for your auction, avoiding traditional paper methods such as checks and money orders. This speeds up transaction times and offers greater security measures to both buyers and sellers. The PayPal payment system has also been designed to detect fraudulent payments in the early stages. If PayPal detects a high-risk payment, you'll receive an email alert telling you the payment has been put into pending status while PayPal investigates. If the payment is legitimate, PayPal will email you letting you know you can ship the item. Fraudulent payments will be cancelled automatically. PayPal offers different levels of accounts for sellers. If you offer PayPal as a payment option, you must accept all forms of PayPal payment. That means you need a premier or business account, personal accounts can only accept three credit card payments before they have to upgrade.

The biggest reason to use PayPal is the sheer number of eBayers that use this payment system. According to a survey 75% of eBayers prefer to use PayPal for their eBay transactions. That makes a Premier or Business Account an essential tool for any successful eBay seller. You've already signed up for PayPal, and you've probably received money too. Until you meet the requirements for offering more payment methods, or something better comes along, PayPal is really the only option you'll need.

b. Accept credit cards

If you want to grow your eBay business, it's essential that you receive credit card payments. You may be able to accept other forms of payment as well, nothing will speed up transactions and help you put your business on autopilot than accepting credit card payments on your eBay auction listings. Credit cards give buyers an added sense of security, and more convenience. Knowing that both PayPal and their credit card provider will protect them in the event of fraud is an important key to overcoming buyer inhibition. You'll need a means of processing cards securely. This involves either setting up a merchant account with a card-issuing bank or using a secure processing service such as PayPal. If you already have a PayPal Personal Account, you can upgrade your account to the Premier Account level in order to receive credit card payments. PayPal charges small fees according to the card your buyers use and the size of your transaction.

c. Escrow service

An escrow service is a licensed and regulated company that collects, holds, and sends a buyer's money to a seller according to instructions agreed on by both the buyer and seller. Escrow is available for any purchase but typically is used for purchases of $500 or more. If you choose to use an escrow service to increase your security on a larger transaction, eBay recommends that you use escrow.com. An escrow puts both buyers and sellers at ease for transactions over $500 and under $5,000. If you participate in the service, the escrow company becomes responsible for verifying every detail of the post-auction process, including - shipping, delivery, payment, and product satisfaction. They mediate the entire transaction from start to finish to reduce risks for both parties. If you choose to use escrow, clearly state that you want your buyers to use the service when they win your items. Escrow.com charges fees for acting as an intermediary. Those fees vary depending on the size of the transaction, and the service level. The buyer and seller negotiate who pays the fees. If the buyer returns the merchandise, yet has agreed to pay the escrow fees, the buyer is still responsible to meet that obligation. The original shipping fee and the escrow fee will be taken out of the initial payment the buyer made to

Escrow.com. Avoid unfamiliar escrow services or ones suggested by your buyers.

d. Other options

Not everyone is comfortable doing business with PayPal, some feel that it gives eBay a little bit too much power over their business, not to mention all the PayPal horror stories out there. Now you can offer ProPay, Moneybookers, or Paymate as electronic payment options for your buyers.

Some eBay members treat eBay as a game and don't care that it's a real marketplace where laws apply. This can be a real problem for sellers. If the winning bidder doesn't pay, an auction can turn into a painful round of bill collecting. To avoid this, set up a system that automatically notifies winning bidders about shipping and handling charges and how you prefer payment. If buyers don't pay after successive requests, notify eBay and relist the auction. eBay will not charge you listing fees for this process, and will proceed with an Unpaid Item Dispute to force delinquent buyers to pay what they owe. If buyers don't respond to the dispute process, eBay could suspend or de-register their account. If a non-payer leaves you negative Feedback, you can have it removed from your profile once it's gone through the dispute process.

B. Packing and insurance

Take some time to figure out how you can address some of the most problematic issues that arise when an eBay auction closes. The more problems you prevent, the better. Especially since the Feedback system lets buyers rate you specifically on your shipping and those ratings count toward how much exposure your listings will get.

a. Shipping plans

These are the most important factors to remember when you develop a shipping plan -

- Quick shipping
- Careful shipping
- Inexpensive shipping
- International shipping
- Tracking
- Insurance

The best way to avoid any kind of problem or communication issue with your bidders is to make a statement that outlines your shipping and payment policies in simple, concrete detail. Include that statement on your About Me page and on all your auction listings. The simpler your statement, the easier it will be to understand for those who might not speak your language. This is especially important if you intend to sell and ship internationally. A clear statement also prevents you from having to answer tons of questions via email. It is another level of protection on your end in case a transaction goes awry.

b. Effective packaging and shipping

Your positive Feedback and Detailed Seller Ratings depends on getting your items to your customers undamaged and in good time. You also need to make certain that your shipping process is as cost-efficient as possible.

a. Give customers all the information

Your customers will want to know the service you are using to deliver their package. Include the carrier and the class of service you intend to use in all your listings. Be conscious of costs to ship to different zones within North America. Before you begin to sell, you want to have all the information you need for all the countries you plan to sell to. Make your shipping policies very clear, and try to anticipate as many buyer questions as possible in advance.

b. Look for ways to save money

When you go to get your supplies for shipping you can do a few things to make sure your costs don't eat into your profit margin -

- Get all the "freebies" you can from your courier or postal services
- Buy the rest of what you need on eBay
- Buy your packaging supplies in bulk
- Use recycled materials
- If a buyer wins more than one item with you, try to ship the items together

Some sellers will offer a base price for shipping and then add a small incremental fee for any other products their buyers want added to that same shipment.

c. Dos and Don'ts

DO -

- Use high-quality cardboard boxes
- Use Microfoam, Sealed Air, low-density bubble wrap, or some form of recycled foam or plastic air-cell packaging

- Give your package a firm shake in a few different directions to see how the packing materials handle it Always double-up on tape or sealant
- Always secure your shipping label with a layer of clear tape or use self sticking shipping labels

DON'T -

- Use newspaper for packing material
- Cushion items with materials that will settle during the shipping process
- Re-use boxes too often
- Think that writing Fragile on an item is going to cause anyone to treat it with more care
- Skimp on padding

Some of the most common mistakes in the shipping process involve not going the extra mile to make sure a package is truly secure. If you are unsure how to ship an item, look for a seller who specializes in that item. Pose as a customer and ask them how they ship their items. You may even want to purchase an item or two so you can see for yourself how other sellers package difficult items.

d. Create a shipping assembly line

Create a defined shipping area and always use it. It can be a whole room or a corner of the garage, even just a table with some shelves next to it. Set up your supplies in a line that reflects the order in which things need to happen. Once you've nailed down a shipping system, you'll be rewarded with higher profits and more time to spend creating listings and sourcing products. You'll encourage positive feedback from pleased buyers who receive your packages at fast for the lowest price.

e. Print labels for shipping

Clear, professional labeling is another important part of packaging your items for mailing. Most auction management software includes a shipping label printing function, as do most other major shipping and mailing organizations. Print labels for the outside of your packages, as well as an additional label to go on the inside in case the outside of the package is damaged or defaced somehow. Even if the external label is lost, your package can be recovered to you or the buyer via the internal label. The easiest option when you're starting out is to print your labels through eBay or PayPal.

Duties or tariffs are charged on certain items when they are shipped out of the country. You will need to attach the appropriate forms to the outside of the package so that customs officials can easily examine them. These forms should be available at your local postal outlet or at the website for your postal service. Always put as much information as possible both on the inside and outside of your package to prevent losses and confusions if the packaging somehow becomes ripped, stained, damaged, or defaced. It is the seller's responsibility to track and monitor the shipping of a product after it has been purchased. To cover your bases as a seller, you should only ship to verified addresses and always track the shipment. Give the tracking number to your buyer so they know exactly when they can expect their purchase. They'll see that it's not you holding up the delivery. PayPal will not cover the seller if there is no tracking or if the item was shipped to an address that has not been verified.

C. **Shipping tools**

You want to make sure every package you send arrives as quickly as possible. When you go to choose your best shipping option, high speed and low cost should be your two biggest priorities.

a. Mail and courier

You can get started by registering for free with all the major courier and mailing organizations that ship both domestically and internationally. The post office is usually your most inexpensive and most convenient option. Keep an eye out for promotions, the USPS has pages of shipping labels, customs forms, international envelopes, and domestic shipping boxes available free and they offer free pick-up. Royal Mail in the UK and Canada Post are two other postal services that have promotions trying to earn the business of eBay sellers. We recommend that you find out what your post office can do for you. To see what special deals eBay has set up with your national post office, search shipping on your local eBay website or go to SellerCentral for your country's eBay and look at the shipping section.

For the United States Postal Service, the mail classifications are based on three factors - the weight of what you are mailing, the size of what you are mailing, and the speed at which you want the package to arrive at its destination. Here are the delivery times for each mail class -

- Express Mail - 1 to 2 days guaranteed delivery, cost based on weight (70 lbs or less) and distance
- Priority Mail - 1 to 3 days guaranteed delivery, costs based on weight and distance if over one pound (70 lbs or less)
- First Class Mail - 1 to 3 days guaranteed delivery, costs based on weight (13 oz. or less) and shape
- Parcel Post - 2 to 9 days guaranteed delivery, costs based on weight and

distance (70 lbs or less)
- Media Mail - 2 to 9 days guaranteed delivery; costs based on weight and content, printed materials such as books, periodicals, magazines, and educational items, as well as some CDs and DVDs for educational use (70 lbs or less)
- Bound Printed Matter - 2 to 9 days guaranteed delivery, costs based on weight, content, and distance (15 lbs or less)

Depending on how quickly you want your item to arrive, there are usually a number of shipping options for any given product. The best solutions are those that balance cost and speed of delivery.

b. Parcel2Go

You might want to check out Parcel2Go, a UK-based delivery company that offers worldwide delivery through couriers like FedEx and DHL. They're offering eBay sellers worldwide a 5% discount just for adding the Parcel2Go logo to auction listings. Parcel2Go offers comprehensive shipping tools and services on their website for sellers making five or more deliveries per day. If you currently send your eBay packages by courier, you'll want to check out Parcel2Go.

The US Postal Service also offers Priority Mail Flat Rate Boxes at a fixed price, with a maximum package weight of 70lbs, regardless of destination -

- Priority Mail Flat Rate Envelope - $4.95, 12.5 x 9.5 inches
- Priority Mail Small Flat-Rate Box - $4.95, 8.625 x 5.375 x 1.625 inches
- Priority Mail Regular Flat-Rate Box (FRB1) - $10.35, 11 x 8.5 x 5.5 inches
- Priority Mail Regular Flat-Rate Box (FRB2) - $10.35, 13.625 x 11.875 x 3.375 inches
- Priority Mail Large Flat-Rate Box (Domestic Addresses) - $13.95, 12.25 x 12.25 x 6 inches
- Priority Mail Large Flat-Rate Box (APO/FPO Destinations) - $11.95, 12.25 x 12.25 x 6 inches

The US Postal Service asks Priority Mail Flat Rate Box users to make sure that all box edges are securely fastened, and that the products included do not stress the packaging. US Postal Service customers can use Click-N-Ship, offered online to print a shipping label and pay the postage. Customers can also use Carrier Pickup online notification to let their post office know they have a package to be collected when their letter carrier delivers their mail the following day.

D. eBay Shipping policies

Out of the many pages of eBay policies, there are only two that you need to know concerning shipping.

a. Item Location Misrepresentation Policy

eBay requires all sellers be truthful and accurate when listing the locations of the seller and the location of the items. If you're using a drop shipper who's located in Tokyo you have to say so. Failure to disclose this important fact can lead to extra customs and duty charges for your buyer, negative Feedback for you, and a range of actions taken by eBay including -

- Listing cancellation
- Forfeit of eBay fees on cancelled listings
- Limits on account privileges
- Loss of PowerSeller status
- Account suspension

This policy is part of the more general rule of demanding truthful, accurate information from sellers. It makes eBay a better place for buyers and sellers.

b. Excessive Shipping Charges Policy

The other part of eBay rules that affects shipping is eBay's no cheating rule, listings cannot use techniques to avoid or circumvent eBay fees. One way sellers tried to do this was charging $1 for a hundred dollar item plus $99 for shipping. That's a BIG no-no. If you're losing money on the item cost and trying to make up for it with shipping and handling, or your shipping charges are higher than your competition's, you'd better rethink your business model. Besides being against the rules, charging excessive shipping will only push your item farther and farther down on the Best Match listing. If you're selling items in the Books, DVDs & Movies, Music, or Video Games categories, you must also be aware that there are maximum shipping and handling costs that you can charge. You must offer at least one shipping option that costs the same or less than the maximum.

7. Test and Track

A. __Understand testing__

If you test you're going to increase the number of people who visit, watch, and then bid on your auctions, ultimately driving up the final selling price of your item. Testing will help you -

- Increase your visitor-to-bid rate
- Increase the overall selling success of your items
- Increase the number of watchers
- Increase customer base and traffic
- Increase profits

Testing on eBay can take some time especially if you're running seven-day auctions but once you see the difference a new auction title or item description can make, you'll love testing. Testing works best if you're selling the same or at least very similar products. Don't assume that just because Buy It Now pricing works for one item, it will work for every item you plan on selling. You still need to test pricing on your other products before you decide to adopt it universally. Most sellers on eBay sell a lot of different items, and since it can be difficult to maintain a control test in eBay's changing sales environment, testing can be tough to gauge accurately on eBay.

The key thing to remember with all types of testing is to change only one element at a time so you always know exactly what's responsible for any improvement. If you change your description at the same time as you change the length of your auction and your photos, you'll never know which change is responsible for your improved results. It could be that the new description may have raised your final sales price by 20%, but the other changes lowered it by 10%. Without having isolated each change, you might assume your new description improved your sales by only 10%, and never realize you're leaving money on the table.

You need to choose a control auction. A control auction is more or less the starting point for your testing, and it becomes the standard against which all test results are compared. To generate your control auction, try three or four different versions of a listing and choose the one that generates the best results. This version will then become your control auction, which you'll start to change slightly over the course of testing. Once you have chosen a control auction, the real testing can begin.

a. Same listing, different title

Take your control auction and change only the title. This simple change can produce dramatic results. Keep tweaking your title until more people start clicking through to your item description. Once you get more people clicking through, you should see a corresponding increase in sales. If your sales results with your new title don't improve, even though more people are now clicking through to your description, this could mean You're attracting untargeted visitors or Your product description is not doing a good job of selling your item.

If you're attracting untargeted visitors, you'll need to keep refining your title until you're getting your best potential customers to your auctions. Remember to pay close attention to how your title changes affect your ranking in the Best Match search results. If you think your title is attracting the right crowd, then it's time to focus on getting more bidders.

b. Same listing, different description

Depending on the item you're selling, the length and quality of your product description can play a large part in your success. Many so-called online auction experts claim that long descriptions don't get read but this is not always the case. When you're selling high-value or unique items you need that extra, persuasive text to convince your potential customers that your offer really is the best. You also need to explain to your readers why you are the best person for them to buy from, and why you are trustworthy as a seller. Remember, your product description needs to sell your item, not just describe it.

c. Same listing, different starting bids

Testing different starting bids is easy but remember that a workable pricing strategy is essential to the success of your auctions. To test, simply take your control auction and change only your starting bid. Run a test auction with a 99-cent starting bid. In a separate test, try out a starting bid that at least covers your costs, and see which generates a higher profit. Don't forget that higher starting bids raise your eBay listing fees, so keep that in mind when comparing your final results. Other pricing strategies you should test include Buy It Now and the use of reserve prices. It's important to realize that you can't launch a handful of tests for the same product simultaneously. Listing too many auctions at the same time can saturate the market and change your selling conditions.

Buyers may also be suspicious if they see numerous auctions for the same product being run by the same seller, but with radically different starting bids and descriptions. To steer clear of these problems, run only one or two tests at the same time, and wait at least a few hours between posting the listings. Because Best Match ranks your items depending on a variety of factors like price, you should also make a careful note of which pricing places your item higher in the search listings as well.

B. Stats to track

If your testing is going to have an impact on your sales, you have to be able to measure the results. These are the statistics you need to be tracking and analyzing.

a. Elements of your auction listings

To ensure you have the information and statistics needed to analyze your results, always maintain detailed records of all your eBay transactions. This will not only provide you with instant Feedback on each of your auctions, but also help you to identify any long-term trends that may develop over time. eBay keeps track of quite a few statistics on the auction listings themselves, which makes finding them easy. To really know how well your listings are working, you need to track and analyze -

- Auction format
- Details of listing
- Number of visitors to your auction
- Number of watchers on your auction
- Number of bids on your auction
- Final selling price of each item
- Number of listings that result in a sale

When you're just starting out, it's easy to find and track this information using your My eBay page. But when your eBay business grows, and you start listing hundreds of auctions a month, you're going to want to consider using some software to help make the job of tracking these statistics easier. eBay's Sales Reports Plus offers a software tool that will assist you in collecting your data and it's free. With Sales Reports Plus you'll receive information on a weekly and monthly basis to better understand your business.

b. Number of visitors to your auctions

The first statistic to focus on is the number of people visiting your auction. The main factors that affect this number are your title, Gallery photo, and the use of any listing upgrades such as bold, highlight, or border. Try to find the combination of these elements that gets the most people visiting your auctions and then later on you can worry about getting them to bid with compelling descriptions and attractive starting bids. Don't forget to take into consideration the costs involved with using listing upgrades.

c. Conversion rates of your auctions

Getting eBay shoppers to open your listings is just half of the battle; you'll want to analyze how your other auction features are affecting the final sales price. Your product description will have a major influence on bidding activity. Other elements, such as your starting bid and the photo quality, will have a major impact as well. Test each of these elements separately over time to determine the best overall listing for your product. The most valuable statistic you'll want to constantly monitor is your conversion rate of visitors to bids. The visitor-to-bid conversion rate allows you to evaluate the number of visitors you actually convert into bids. Once you get your conversion rate to a level you are happy with, you can again focus on bringing more interested visitors to your item description. Since your conversion rates should stay the same, more visitors will mean more sales.

To calculate your visitor-to-bid conversion rate, use this formula -

Number of Bids / Number of Visitors x 100 = Visitor-to-Bid Conversion Rate

If your control auction gets 100 visitors and 30 bids, then your visitor-to-bid conversion rate is 30% -

30 / 100 x 100 = 30%

The higher the visitor-to-bid conversion rate, the more successful your auction will be. A high rate indicates that you're attracting visitors who are interested in bidding on your product, and your salescopy and pictures are enticing them to bid. Another way of looking at this information is by dividing your visitors by your bids to see the ratio of visitors to bids. Testing will give you a sense of what conversion rates are good for your business.

d. Sell-through rate

A final statistic every seller on eBay needs to monitor is the percentage of listings that result in a sale. This is called your sell-through rate. Approximately 45% of all eBay auctions end in a sale, this number varies among different items. The fact is that sell-through rates will differ according to your market and what you're selling but always keep an eye on this figure and constantly try to improve it. Increasing your items' sell-through rates will not only increase your profits, it will also save you time, as you'll have fewer items to relist. Plus, it will save you from paying listing fees for items that don't sell.

C. <u>Tracking tools</u>

As we said testing will do you no good unless you're able to learn from it. For that to happen, you'll need to record all your tests and what you learn from them. Using the Testing & Tracking Spreadsheet and your Testing Worksheet for eBay Listings you'll be tracking the following statistics -

- Test strategy
- URLs and Titles of auctions being tested
- Category
- Placement in Best Match results
- Number of visitors
- Number of watchers
- Number of bids
- Starting price
- Ending price
- Sold or not sold
- Terapeak average price for this item
- How much higher (or lower) than the average the item sold for
- Visitor-to-bid conversion rate

If your listing's profit margin increases even by a single percentage point, you're headed in the right direction. Your strategy is to keep testing one change at a time until you find the perfect recipe to sell your items effectively and efficiently. Two tools you could use to track your performance metrics are eBay Sales Reports and Terapeak. eBay offers two levels of free Sales Reports - the basic level is available to sellers with 10 or more Feedback who've completed one successful sale within the last four months. While any seller with an eBay account in good standing can sign up for Sales Reports Plus. Sales Reports is recommended for low-to-medium sellers who want sales and fee summaries. Sales Reports Plus works best if you move a lot of product and want more in-depth information to help you design your sales strategies.

D. <u>10 critical elements</u>

In the online auction format, you can, and should, test all the different options that eBay makes available to you when creating your listings, all the time, paying attention to how each change affects your rankings in Best Match search. Once you've got your control listing and you're following your statistics, you can start changing different elements -

a. Your offer

Your offer is the total package you're selling. It includes your main item plus any incentive items you may have included. Try changing your offer by emphasizing different benefits or including a couple of bonus items.

b. Auction title

Your auction title appears in the eBay search results, and it's the first place where you get to distinguish yourself from your competitors. Your title will have a huge impact on the response your auctions receive. It's what initially captures shopper's attention and compels them to visit your auction, so it pays to spend some time working on it.

Remember, the words you choose for your title need to match the keywords people are using to search for items on eBay or your listing will never even be seen. Some of the key features of a title you should be testing include the keywords, the use of brand names, the use of abbreviations, and the use of different descriptive words for your product.

c. Using subtitles

We recommend the use of subtitles only in specific situations, such as adding incentives like free shipping during the holidays. Try out a few different subtitles at different times of the year to see if they bring more people to your auctions. Don't forget that subtitles are not searchable when someone does a basic search by title only, so you don't need to focus on filling your subtitle with keywords. The purpose of any subtitle you test should be purely to persuade as many viewers as possible to click through to your auction listing.

d. eBay Listing Features

Bold, border, and highlight are listing upgrades that can be purchased to increase your item's visibility in the search results page. Because you have to pay for these upgrades, you must test carefully before deciding to use them on a larger scale. They could be just the boost your listing needs to attract the attention of shoppers on eBay. These upgrades are easy to test, just run listings with and without them around the same time, then compare.

e. Gallery Plus image

Gallery images are free, so including one with your listings is a given. People want to be able to see your item to decide whether they want to buy it and they don't want to have to take the extra step to click through to your listing to see it. Why not test the enhanced version, Gallery Plus. When someone mouses over a listing that uses Gallery Plus, an enlarged version of the Gallery photo pops up, covering nearby listings. Test hosting your photos through eBay Picture Services when you use Gallery Plus versus a free third-party hosting. Even though eBay charges you per photo, when you use Gallery Plus, searchers will be able to see enlarged versions of an entire listing directly from the search results page.

f. Product description

Tweak your product description continually until it's the most descriptive it can be. Consider adding some testimonials or moving around any photos within your description. Try out both short and long copy, and think back to the tips you learned when you wrote your first item descriptions. Test the auction a few times with one change and track the responses you get.

g. Pricing strategies

Determining your optimum pricing strategy will be one of the most difficult aspects of creating successful auction listings. The only surefire way to find out if you should start the bidding on your auctions low, high, or with a BIN option is to run some tests. Eventually you'll get a feel for what prices will attract the most bidders to your products. Conventional wisdom on eBay is to start the bidding low in an attempt to generate interest and create a bidding frenzy, but sometimes starting it high can increase the perceived value of your product and bring you more profits in the end. Others find that the Buy It Now option brings them more profits than through bidding, particularly if they're selling mass-produced items.

h. Number of photos

Having great pictures is one of the key elements of your sales process. They play a major role not only in generating more bids, but also in raising the final sales price. So make sure to run some test auctions with different numbers of photos to measure the impact they have your sales. One of the main drawbacks for people shopping on eBay is that they can't physically inspect the items they are interested in. To help alleviate this situation, it's crucial that you give prospective bidders as many views of your items as possible. Taking top-quality pictures of the items you're selling can take a lot of time and effort.

i. Duration and timing

Make sure that you are testing different auction lengths for all your items. Your auction will also get the most attention the first day it's posted and a few hours before it ends. Think about your target market, look at the busiest times on your auctions and try starting and ending your auctions at different times and on different days.

j. Design elements

Product descriptions need to be scannable, which means visitors to your auctions can easily see the key messages of your product description just by scanning the listing instead of having to read every word. To make your auction scannable, ensure that your headline is a larger font than the rest of your text, highlight or bold certain key features in different colors, and don't forget to include bullet point lists that outline the benefits of your product. Design elements such as these will pop off the screen and be easy for potential customers to read.

These are just some of the variables you can test. Try testing the different listing upgrades, discounts, best offer, and all the other options eBay offers. Knowledge is power. Testing and tracking your results can give you exclusive access to the kind of powerful knowledge that can have an impact on your business. To truly be successful on eBay, you must test everything you can, and test often. Unless you do, you'll never know how much profit you're letting slip through your fingers. Testing isn't a one-time thing. Make a point of testing at least one key element of your auctions every week. This may seem like a lot of work right now, but when you see your first test that genuinely makes a difference in sales, you'll see that it's all worthwhile.

Chapter Three

Feedback and Automating Business

1. Your Feedback Rating

A. Understand the Feedback system

Good service, appealing prices, quality products, and a consistently positive shopping experience are the basic factors that keep shoppers coming back. The same rules apply to the shopping experience on eBay with one difference. On eBay there isn't any face-to-face contact between you and your customers. Online shoppers need information they can use to evaluate whether you will deliver what you promise or simply disappear into the sunset with their money. The way they'll decide if you're reputable and trustworthy is by looking at your Positive Feedback Percentage and Detailed Seller Ratings. A good profile is an important part of doing business on eBay. Listings are ranked according to the seller's Detailed Seller Ratings. Creating a positive customer experience has never been more important. Once you know how you'll be rated, you can take steps to keep your feedback profile in good standing.

Your Feedback profile consists of a Feedback Score, a Positive Feedback Percentage, and Detailed Seller Ratings. At the end of every transaction, buyers are encouraged to leave Feedback for sellers. They have up to 60 days after a transaction, they can rate their satisfaction with the experience by -

- Leaving a positive (+1), neutral (0), or a negative (-1) Feedback score. Negative scores count against the seller when positive Feedback percentage is calculated
- Writing a single line of text to explain their reason for leaving a particular piece of Feedback
- Detailed Seller Ratings rate sellers out of five stars in four areas - item

description, communication, shipping times, and shipping charges

Sellers are limited to leaving either positive Feedback or no Feedback for buyers, along with a short comment. We recommend that you wait to leave positive Feedback for your buyers until you receive payment. Once payment is received, send a thank-you message including the expected arrival time and a request for positive Feedback. This will encourage your buyers to leave positive Feedback, and will make them much more likely to give you a good DSR in Communication.

a. Feedback

Your Feedback Score is the total number of Feedback points you have received in the last 12 months. Your Positive Feedback percentage is the total number of positive Feedback points you've received, expressed as a percentage of your total Feedback. A perfect Feedback rating will appear as 100%. Your Feedback percentage is based on a 12-month period only, negatives won't permanently affect your record.

Your Feedback rating is indicated by the star symbol that appears next to most user names. Different colors indicate various levels of achievement, letting eBay users see at a glance how well established and trustworthy you are. Once you achieve a minimum Feedback score of 10, you are awarded a yellow star. At 50, you receive a blue star, and so on. it goes. Learn more about Feedback scores and stars on the eBay site.

b. Detailed Seller Ratings

Although a high positive Feedback percentage can unlock some doors for you, your Detailed Seller Ratings (DSRs) are your real key to success. Buyers can rate a seller from 1 (terrible) to 5 (excellent) in each of the four DSR categories -

- Item Description
- Communication
- Shipping Time
- Shipping and Handling Charges

So why do these ratings matter so much?

- If you're a regular seller, your DSRs help determine your listing position in eBay's search results.
- If you want to be a PowerSeller, DSRs largely determine your eligibility.
- If you're already a PowerSeller, high DSRs save you money on fees.
- If you want to take advantage of the biggest fee discounts and best ranking in the search results, top-notch DSRs with less than 1% 1s and 2s make you

a Top-rated Seller.

Low DSRs provide a more accurate measure of the quality of a seller's service. That's because buyers might have different ideas of what constitutes a good rating. Some buyers might think a 4 out of 5 is a good rating, but for eBay anything lower than a 4.3 average doesn't make the cut. Sellers will be encouraged to focus on avoiding 1- and 2-star ratings than on getting more 5s to increase their overall average. eBay penalizes sellers who have 1- or 2-star ratings for more than 1% of their transactions.

This works well for small home-based eBay businesses that take the time to communicate with their customers and provide stellar service. It makes it easier for them to compete against the corporate giants that sell a high volume of goods without paying much attention to their customer service. Only domestic DSRs count toward a seller's ratings. Too many sellers have complained about getting low ratings on shipping and delivery due to circumstances beyond their control. By looking only at domestic DSRs, eBay hopes to eliminate this problem. Your Seller Dashboard has a tool that lets you see a daily snapshot of how you measure up to the new low DSR requirement, so make sure you check it regularly to see how you're doing.

B. Building good Feedback

Building up your Feedback profile can seem like a daunting task to an eBay newbie. There are strategies you can use to build your rating and earn your first star. It's important when you're getting started to let people know why they can trust you, and why you're qualified to sell what you sell. The best way to show you're trustworthy is to prove it by building your Feedback score.

a. Become a buyer

When you're starting out, you can start building your Feedback score and comments by buying some low-cost items on eBay. This won't get you started developing any detailed seller ratings or seller-specific Feedback but it will put you on the road to collecting your first star and proving that you're a reliable person to do business with. Right from your first bid, be a great buyer. Make your payments on time and be friendly and courteous to all sellers. Once each transaction has been completed to your satisfaction, leave positive Feedback and ask the seller to return the favor if they haven't already.

b. Build your rating

Successfully complete as many transactions as you can in the early days. Selling small, inexpensive items that can be shipped quickly is a great way to establish your reputation as a reliable seller and encourage top DSRs. Make sure you ask for feedback for every transaction you perform well.

c. Be the seller you would want to buy from

Respond quickly to customer emails and inquiries, ship items promptly and carefully, and be professional and courteous in all your interactions.

d. About Me and My World pages

Share information about yourself and your experience, as well as any other ventures that can strengthen your credibility as a seller. You are permitted to link to your off-eBay site as long as you don't break the links policy.

e. Resolve any disputes quickly and effectively

Remember that on eBay, the customer is always right. Encourage your customers to contact you if they are not 100% happy with their purchase so you can make it right. Buyers are able to reverse their Feedback if they believe they're made a mistake or if the issue is resolved.

f. Legal obligations

As with any business, you need to know the rules of the game if you're going to get ahead. As an eBay seller, you must be aware of these guidelines -

- You are required to ship items within the time frame specified during your auction
- Your item description must state that that your photo is not the actual item you're selling if you use a stock photo.

Visit these pages for a full overview of eBay's rules and regulations -

- eBay policies overview
- Rules for sellers
- Feedback rules

Now more than ever before, you need to do everything you can to avoid negative Feedback, especially low DSRs. Many eBay services, benefits, and opportunities are only available to sellers with high positive Feedback and DSR ratings. Since eBay introduced Best Match as its default search method, your DSR ratings will determine where your listings appear in the search results. It used to be that when you searched for an item on eBay, the first results you saw were the listings that were ending soonest. Now the results are listed according to a formula that sorts all the possible results according to a combination of factors. It's unclear how these factors are weighed against each other, so it's important that you treat them all as important. These factors will help you rise in the results -

- Relevance
- DSRs of 4.7 or above
- Free shipping

Factors that will cause you to drop -

- Buyer dissatisfaction rates greater than 5%
- Low DSRs for Shipping and Handling charges.
- Above average shipping costs

The time remaining on a listing is still used for auction listings but it isn't the main focus any longer. While your auction listing will probably be near the top in its last few minutes and hours, it might share space with other listings with days to go, listings created by sellers who know how to work the system. The best way to ensure that you're not shoved way out on page 5 with just minutes to spare on your auction is to make sure your DSRs are in good shape. It's easier to prevent bad buyer experiences before they become problems than to try to fix them afterwards.

C. **Be a five star superstar**

Use these strategies to get high DSRs and get your listings to the top of the searches.

a. Item Description

Most buyers leave negative Feedback because they don't receive what they expected. You can make buyers happy by -

- Putting your items in the right category and sub-category
- Describing every item you sell as accurately as possible
- Clearly describing any and all flaws
- Including lots of photographs
- Specifying shipping details
- Anticipating and responding to customer questions.
- Including a money-back guarantee
- Delivering on all promises

Give your bidders all the information they need to make an informed decision and do everything you can to provide buyers with a positive experience. Deliver on your promises, if you overdeliver on expectations you will create happy buyers, and your Feedback will show it.

b. Communication

Communicating with buyers effectively will solve misunderstandings before they arise, help sell your items, and help you get top stars for communication. You can succeed by -

- Being crystal clear about everything
- Using eBay messages and autoresponders
- Answering emails promptly
- Adding a personal touch

Show what you're doing to meet DSR criteria. List the four DSR criteria under their own headings in a Customer Service section of your auctions. Under each heading you can lay out exactly what you do to address these vital areas of a buyer's experience. You can point visitors towards specific Feedback that praises your customer service in these areas. This will help prove that you're a seller who can be trusted.

c. Shipping time

eBay tries to encourage buyers to rate this section only on how long it took the seller to get it in the mail, some insist on holding you responsible for the post office's mistakes via your DSR. To decrease the likelihood of this happening, here are a few tips -

- Set up your shipping center
- Tell the buyer the status of an order
- Track your package
- Use U.S. Postal Service Delivery Confirmation

d. Shipping costs

Charging fair and accurate shipping costs is a must on eBay. Even if you do everything right, some buyers just won't give you five stars. Control what you can control and -

- Make sure you're offering a competitive rate
- Use calculated shipping

- Offer free shipping
- Offer combined shipping discounts
- Offer after-the-sale shipping discounts
- Provide details about any packaging or handling charges

If after doing everything right, you still receive some lower ratings, don't panic. Your DSR is based only on the last 30 days, so you can work to improve it all the time. Make it your business to find out why you're receiving lower scores, so you can adjust your sales process until you hit on your winning formula.

D. <u>Negative Feedback</u>

You respond quickly to customer emails and inquiries. You ship items promptly and carefully. You're professional and courteous in all your interactions. Sometimes, despite your best efforts you get negative feedback. eBay research shows that buyers are more loyal to sellers with whom they've successfully resolved a dispute than they are to ones where no problem has occurred at all. So it's worth learning how to deal with negative Feedback gracefully. Negative feedback can be reversed, Buyers whose complaints have been resolved are able to change both the comment and the Feedback rating they've left. When you resolve a buyer's problem, you often score yourself a customer for life in the process. There are five ways you can handle negative Feedback - .

- Block high-risk buyers from your auctions
- Get abusive Feedback removed immediately
- Talk to your buyer to clear up misunderstandings
- Report troublemakers to eBay
- Respond to Feedback

Your best bet is to try to resolve the issue with the other party directly. You can use eBay's buyer and seller forms to contact them and try to come to a mutual understanding. You might be able to persuade them to leave a follow-up comment that explains the misunderstanding, you might even get them to retract their negative. How you approach the buyer can have a huge effect on the outcome. Use tried-and-true dispute resolution techniques. Focus on the problem, not the person and always give your buyer the benefit of the doubt. If you're diplomatic and try to see things from your customer's perspective, you're far more likely to get the result you want.

E. Feedback automation tools

As you know, one of the most difficult aspects of running your business on eBay is the challenge of finding the time to take care of little tasks. You're busy doing research, sourcing products, creating listings, and filling orders that come in, so as your business ramps up, it can be difficult to keep on top of the little customer service tasks that ensure you get positive Feedback after every transaction. There are automation tools that can help you set up easy automated processes to keep everything running smoothly at the end of each auction -

- eBay's Selling Manager Pro - The basic Selling Manager is free to all eBay sellers and it's a useful tool. The next level up - Selling Manager Pro, you can get a 30-day free trial and compare it to the free version. It lets you automate your processes for Feedback, email, and relisting auctions. Subscriptions start at $15.99 or free if you sign up for a Premium or Anchor store.
- Auctiva - This auction software includes a free Feedback autoresponder that leaves positive Feedback as soon as you receive a positive from a buyer. You can write a variety of messages and the software will cycle through them. You can also get reports on what Feedback you've sent and the buyers you've sent it to. Auctiva charges $2.95 per month for up to 15 listings and $9.95 per month for more than 15 listings.
- Vrane's Auto Feedback Robot - Responds to all positive Feedback that you receive with one of up to 20 comments that you create and store in the member's area. The Robot will notify you if and when you receive neutral or negative Feedback so you can respond. You need to be registered with Vrane in order to use the Auto Feedback Robot and you'll need to purchase credits from them before you can access the tool or any other software they offer.
- Merlin Software's InstantFeedback software - Automatically post positive Feedback for anyone who has left it for you. You can choose pre-made Feedback, or customize it. InstantFeedback will let you know if you receive negative or neutral Feedback. The software costs $19.95 to download, or $24.95 for a CD version.

Using automated Feedback tools is a great way to make sure you always leave Feedback in a timely manner, no matter how many sales you have. Not only does this make you look like a pro, it also encourages your buyers to respond in kind.

F. Feedback milestones

Feedback is an invaluable tool for buyers because it lets you see exactly how well a seller has treated previous customers. It's also key to getting maximum exposure for your listings, as well as unlocking special privileges as your business grows. Maintain high DSRs and great Feedback, and get rewarded at these milestones -

- First sale with or without Feedback - After you've made one sale, eBay will let you open your own store, as long as you have a PayPal account in good standing. Without PayPal, you'll need a Feedback rating of 20
- 5 positive Feedback - You can sell items at a fixed price using the "Buy It Now" feature. Without a PayPal account, you'll need a rating of 10
- 10 positive Feedback - You can use the Best Offer feature on single-item listings.
- 15 positive Feedback - You can sell multiple copies of an item in a single listing using the Fixed Price Listing. Without PayPal, you'll need a rating of 30.
- 20 positive Feedback - Sellers with a Feedback rating of 20 can open an eBay store without a PayPal account.
- 30 positive Feedback - You can accept Best Offers on a Fixed Price Listing. You must have been a registered eBay user for at least 14 days, or be ID Verified, to access this feature.
- 100 positive Feedback - Scoring 100 Feedback, with a 12-month positive Feedback rating of 98% or better, is the first step to turning into a PowerSeller. At 100, you can register as an eBay Trading Assistant to earn commissions by selling other people's stuff.

a. PowerSeller

The best thing about reaching the 100 positive Feedback mark is that you can become a PowerSeller, if you maintain yearly sales over $3,000 and keep your positive Feedback percentage over 98%. You're also required to have maintained a rating of 4.5 or higher for the past 12 months in all four DSRs, with no more than 1% 1- and 2-star ratings. These requirements are soon changing but you can see all the requirements on eBay. Becoming a PowerSeller has rewards like -

- Final Value Fee discounts
- UPS rate discounts
- Welcome kit
- Priority customer service
- Networking opportunities
- Health insurance
- Business stationery templates
- Special offers
- Powerful Giving Program
- Eligibility to become a Top-rated Seller

b. Top-rated Seller

In 2009, eBay created the Top-rated Seller category, a new level of sellers. A top rated seller is fairly new but here's what you have to do to achieve this -

- Average DSR of 4.6
- Maintain a 0.5% percentage of 1- and 2-star ratings
- At least 100 transactions and $3,000 in sales in the past twelve months

That means you have to do everything in your power to make sure your customers all have a positive buying experience which is something you should be working hard to ensure. Here are some rewards for top rated sellers -

- Final Value Fee discounts
- Increased visibility
- Featured First
- Unique icon for your listings

Membership in the PowerSeller and Top-rated Seller programs is free but they are by invitation only, as soon as you qualify, eBay will email you a special invitation to join the program. When you become a PowerSeller, eBay calculates your Feedback score differently from regular sellers and the moment you're accepted into the program, you could see your own score shoot up. Remember you have a Feedback score and a Feedback rating. For regular sellers, feedback score reflects the number of times you've received feedback from unique users, as well as one point a week for buyers who purchase multiple items from you.

That means if you get 10 positive Feedback comments from one customer in a week, your score will only actually increase by one point. When you become a PowerSeller, eBay begins displaying Feedback score based on the total number of Feedback comments you've received. Depending on how many transactions you've made, as soon as you hit the 100 mark and qualify, your displayed score could rocket up.

2. eBay Stores

A. <u>The basics</u>

Automation frees up your time so you can focus on the Big Picture. If you're not worried about all the tiny details of how your business operates day-to-day, you can spend a lot more time figuring out how to take it to the next level. One easy step you can take is to open an eBay store. With the tools eBay provides to store owners, you can create multiple listings; add plenty of images; buy and sell using a trusted shopping cart and checkout system, and contact your buyers at every stage and much more.

eBay Stores are a special part of eBay where sellers can show all their listings at once and establish a business identity through customized pages. Most eBay Stores include store inventory items, fixed-price items not available in regular auction listings on eBay. With an eBay Store, you can offer a whole selection of products in one place, and buyers can find all your merchandise, just by clicking on one item. There are three levels of eBay Stores for sellers -

a. Basic

A Basic Store costs $15.95 per month. You get the essential tools to set up an eBay Store website with multiple listings and 1 megabyte of image hosting. If this is your first time running a store, start here. It's the most cost-effective choice for smaller sellers with a limited product range.

b. Premium

A Premium Store costs $49.95 per month and includes additional tools for medium-volume sellers, 50 MB of image hosting, and listing on the eBay Stores page. Premium stores give you more advanced options as a seller, and better results in the off-eBay search engines. The selling manager is upgraded to Selling Manager Pro as well.

c. Anchor

An Anchor Store costs $299.99 per month, it's exclusively for those looking to aggressively increase their eBay businesses. The Anchor level offers the largest selection of tools and lowest per-item fees for high-volume users, as well as listings that are featured on both eBay Stores and regular eBay pages. This is your best option once you've outgrown the Premium Store and offers the full suite of upgrades.

eBay is dedicated to creating tools that help sellers maximize their profit potential. When you do well, eBay does well, too. That's why you can count on their tools to help you grow your business. Take some time to explore all the options and assistance eBay offers, and save yourself time and money as your business grows in size. Compare store subscriptions and fees in more detail on eBay.

B. <u>Store owner benefits and basic tools</u>

Running an eBay Store isn't any more work than running your auctions normally. A store can save you time and money. It can increase your sales, profit margins, and total revenues. eBay Stores offer many benefits like -

- A virtual storefront that stands out from the competition
- A fixed and personal URL on the Internet
- A cost-effective way to build your business and showcase all your items
- Lower selling costs
- Sales and traffic reports
- Accounting Assistant
- Help Line
- Sales management tools

There are a few drawbacks as well. The most significant drawback is that store items don't get as much exposure in eBay search results as regular auction listings. These tips should help you.

a. Balance store and auction items

Try to have a balance of auctions and store items and then cross-promote the auction items to your store. Make sure that along with your store inventory, you feature similar or identical items in auction format. You don't have to do this for all the different variations you sell but make sure you have at least one that directs traffic to your store to see more variety.

b. Promote your store off eBay

Use a store referral link to promote your store wherever possible. Whenever you bring customers to your store or store items from outside eBay, you save 75% of your final fee value. This can add up and it's easy to do.

c. Use keywords

This will help buyers find your items while searching in your store. Keywords will also help bring bidders searching in the complete eBay listings. Stores are the best way to get the most exposure on eBay. More exposure means more sales. The personalized nature of your store also helps you keep those customers coming back for more, and repeat business is the best kind.

d. Build your Recent Sales figures

A good Recent Sales score gives you a boost in eBay's search results. It's the number of sales of a particular item in the last 30 days. Here are suggestions for improving your Recent Sales score -

- List your multi-quantity inventory in Fixed Price with a 30-day duration
- If you use the Good 'Til Cancelled option your listing will automatically renew every 30 days.
- If your multi-quantity listing sells out or expires, don't create a new listing, add inventory and relist.
- When you relist or revise a listing, don't change the title, item condition, or category, or increase the price. Any of these actions will reset the item's Recent Sales.

Your eBay Store is pretty much your own website. You've got a unique URL and a lot of freedom to customize the design, so take advantage of the many customizable features your store offers. You can personalize the design, create your own logo, publish a uniquely branded newsletter, and spice up the look of all your pages, among other options. We recommend a store to everyone who wants to sell more than the odd hand-me-down. To sign up, go to the eBay Stores homepage. When creating your store, ensure that you have a good name for your store that's different from your user ID, use searchable keywords related to your category and product line.

To start customizing your store, click the Store icon on your seller profile or type the URL of your store directly into your browser's address bar. When you're viewing your store, click the link that says Seller, Manage Store near the bottom right of your store page. Be sure to bookmark your store page for future reference. Keep in mind that your store should accomplish two main goals - It should help drive more traffic to your listings and it should save you money on listing fees. Here's how you can begin customizing -

- Logo - Design your own logo or have one designed for you. You might hire a local graphic designer or you could consider using a web-based template service to design one for you.
- Store description - Try to use all the allowed characters and fill your description with searchable keywords to assist users in finding your store and your items.

- Templates and themes - Take a look through these and choose the one most suited to your business or try your hand at making your own
- Store header - Try using a store header with a bit of a description of your items with keywords
- Item display - View your store with List View and Gallery View and decide which is best for you.
- Store Categories - Create up to 300 categories using keywords that make sense to your customers. They'll show up in whatever order you wish, and you can change the order when you want. Don't worry if you don't have any items listed there yet. This won't be shown to buyers unless you have a listing in that category.
- Promotion Boxes - Create some boxes you can place around your store and use them to promote items, display graphics, have buyers sign-up for your newsletter, etc.
- Listing header - The listing header will show up on all your listings and can be used to promote your store, display your logo, and get people to sign up for your newsletter.
- Search engine keywords - By default eBay pulls these from your listings in each category. Monitor these and change them to the keywords that will work best so you'll get the most exposure outside eBay.
- Listing feeds - Turn both of them on to get even more off eBay exposure.
- Cross-promotions - Go in and update cross-promotions preferences to get more exposure with your items.
- Selling Manager - Free with your store, subscribing to Selling Manager will give you more control over your listings.
- Custom Pages - Use this feature to create additional store pages. Some ideas may be to showcase or display specific items or product lines to make the most of your keywords. You can also use custom pages to create a Store Policies page, promote specials, show off your About Me page, or do just about anything else, as long as it's allowed by eBay.
- HTML Builder - eBay will help you create links to store items, searches, and categories that you can use in your listings. If you have any sites or pages outside eBay, you can create links to your store and put them up.

Keep adding items to your store and test listings, layouts and price points. Some items may sell quickly while others may take more time. This is a low-cost investment which, over time, should prove to be profitable or at least educational. If an item doesn't sell on auction or relisting, put it in your store and test different price points including higher than your starting bid, lower than your starting bid, and Best Offer. Visit eBay's Selling with eBay Stores page for more information.

To gain some free exposure for your store, submit it to PayPal's Shops directory, it's free. If you've got a Premier or Business account, a verified account with a credit card, and a seller reputation of 10 or greater, you can submit your site.

C. <u>Advanced tools</u>

Once you've created a store and become comfortable with the basics, you'll find more tools and opportunities available to you as an eBay Store owner. Here are a few -

- Use the traffic and sales reports for more info on your customers.
- Send email promotions via the store e-mail promotion to those who ask for your newsletter and mark you as a favorite seller.
- Create a promotional paper flyer on eBay to include with shipments.
- Get a Seller Outreach tune-up. Seller Outreach is a program where a representative will review your listings and eBay Store with you and help provide easy, actionable suggestions on how you can increase your effectiveness on eBay.
- Visit the eBay Stores Discussion Board for best practices and ideas from other store owners.
- If you're going away for a while, make sure you're aware of the options for your store so your customers know that you're temporarily unavailable. Set up a vacation message in your listings, in your store, or just make your listings unavailable while you're away.
- Upgrade your store to get more exposure and options. Once you've had your Basic store up and running, and are looking to grow bigger, you might want to check out the Premium and Anchor store possibilities.
- Have a sale with Markdown Manager: Discount products or shipping easily and display your special offers when they're in effect.

Once you've set up your store, you don't have to wait days or weeks for the sales to come before analyzing your store. Critique your own store the day you set it up. The first step is to open your store page. Look at it for 10 seconds and run through this checklist -

- Does it make you want to stay and shop?
- Is the page easy to read?
- Is it an appealing layout?
- Is the theme suitable to your image and products?
- What about the color? Is it a good use of color and not too loud? Is it an appealing and appropriate contrast?
- Is the page neat and organized with no clutter?
- Does the list or gallery view suit the design?
- Is the search box easy to find?
- Is it an appropriate store name with keywords?
- Does your logo look professional?
- Are the custom categories keyword-rich and nicely organized?

- Are the Promo Boxes (product promotion, policies, newsletter signup) present and well-placed?
- On your opt-in offers, is there a call to action?
- Do you have a place for shoppers to sign up for your newsletter?
- Can your visitors easily add you to their favorite sellers list and bookmark your store?
- Are the RSS feeds turned on?

Once you've looked at your store and identified any weaknesses, you can start making improvements. It may never be perfect but every step you take will get you that much closer to the eBay business of your dreams.

3. eBay Automation Tools

A. <u>What can you automate?</u>

When you're starting out and only selling a few items at a time, it's easy to stay on top of the process of creating and monitoring listings, receiving payment, shipping, and leaving Feedback. Once you've ramped up your business and you're on your way to being a high-volume seller, you could find yourself spending your whole day managing email and other details instead of working on growing your business and profits. You've already run enough auctions to know how much time it can take that's why you need to automate all those repetitive tasks and spend your time finding more product to sell.

Automation is the real key to success on eBay and when you get those daily tasks running themselves right from the beginning, you're set up for success. Automating your eBay business will allow you to expand and grow more than any traditional business could possibly manage. Using the tools and strategies laid out you'll be able to make your eBay business grow the way you dreamed. Get into the habit of automating your tasks now so that when your sales start to take off, the manual chores won't slow you down, and you can take your business to the next level. You can't automate everything but eBay offers a wide variety of tools that can handle many of your daily eBay tasks and chores. As the eBay community continues to grow more software developers are turning their attention to creating technology for this growing market. Some work for eBay, others develop tools outside eBay and become eBay Certified Providers. Using these tools, you can quickly automate some of your most time-intensive chores. Review this list and consider how much time each could save you -

- Design professional-looking auction listings - Just plug your details into a template and set up effective auction listings that are proven sellers. If you use templates with a consistent look and feel, you'll start developing a recognizable brand that your customers will begin to associate with.
- List more auctions at a time on eBay - Keep your auctions humming by automatically uploading what you need to sell, when you choose to sell it. Once you've drafted a listing, you can pre-program your uploader to place it for auction on a certain date, at a certain time.
- Relist for better Best Match results - When you relist a multi-quantity item, you retain all the stats you've collected while it was listed previously. This is the easiest way to keep your listing moving up in the search results.
- Monitor your auction activity - Whether you're buying or selling, there are tools that can keep track of what's going on in your auctions. They report the details back to you in simple formats that are easy to understand and quick to process.
- Automatically follow up with your subscribers by email - Keep your

potential customers up to date and informed about current auctions, upcoming auctions, their transactions, and other projects that they might be interested in.

- Manage your budgets and finances - Keep your finances in good order and forecast your future profits. Upload a shipping costs calculator or auction fees calculator to help you with daily and monthly expense budgeting.
- Manage your auctions remotely - Stay plugged in to your auctions and your store, without being stuck at your desk. Wireless auction software can keep you in the loop and connected to your business, no matter where you go.
- Cut your research time in half - Market research, reporting, and forecasting programs can help you investigate niche markets, keywords, categories, and what's hot on eBay.
- Calculate shipping on the spot - Never get stuck with a high shipping charge because you estimated the costs of mailing your products, use the shipping calculator in all listings.

B. Recommended eBay tools

eBay has developed a lot of tools to help sellers succeed and many are free. You may find that you'll outgrow these tools as your business grows larger, and you need more robust automation products to handle your growing needs. Here are the most effective tools we've found -

1. Turbo Lister - This free desktop tool is designed to help ease the stress of creating multiple listings. You can list items all at once, as well as save listings to reuse again and again. Turbo Lister features convenient HTML templates and gives you the ability to create listings easily.
2. eBay Toolbar - Features desktop alerts and quick access to eBay areas, gives you the ability to view the top items you're buying and selling.
3. Selling Manager - This tool that gives you access to email and Feedback templates, bulk Feedback processing, bulk relisting capability, printable templates for invoices and shipping labels, downloadable sales history, bulk unpaid item dispute filing and more.
4. Selling Manager Pro - This is the feature-rich version of Selling Manager and offers inventory management, listing statistics, numerous bulk features, automated email, reporting, and listing-designers and templates. You can use the program to schedule your auction listings, automate bulk Feedback postings, print shipping labels, and automatically create sales reports. Selling Manager Pro is available for $15.99 a month and is free if you have a Premium or Anchor store.
5. eBay Blackthorne Basic - Offers features like bulk listing, bulk post-sales management, and local data storage. The monthly fee for the service is $9.99, but a 30-day free trial is offered.

6. eBay Blackthorne Pro - Offers all the features of Blackthorne Basic, plus an open database, inventory management, monthly sales reports, filters and macros, picture management, and multi-user profiles. The monthly fee for the service is $24.99, but a 30-day free trial is available.

7. Accounting Assistant - Works with your existing QuickBooks setup and exports eBay and PayPal transaction and fee data to QuickBooks. Accounting Assistant is free for all eBay Store owners and for subscribers to Selling Manager, Selling Manager Pro, or any of the Blackthorne packages.

8. Markdown Manager - Available to eBay Store owners, this tool lets you highlight and clear out old inventory items by putting them on sale. This is a good way to build customer loyalty, you can promote your sales using email or your newsletter and bring customers and opt-ins back to your site.

If you plan to take your eBay business beyond the point where you are selling just a few items out of your basement, it's important that you automate as many tasks as you can from the beginning. Pay close attention to what automation tools the top PowerSellers on eBay are using, but make sure any tool you're considering could work effectively for you. Check around in forums and discussion groups to gather Feedback on the software or tools you are considering for your auction business. Ask questions, read ratings and reviews, and use that information to pick the best tools for you.

C. <u>Third party software</u>

Most auction management software was invented for use on eBay, and most of the industry still remains primarily eBay-focused. It makes sense that the developers would aim for the largest market available, and their attention to eBay's specific needs works to your benefit. Often, these tools offer more detailed support and information in specific areas, combined with sophisticated auction management interfaces. New software for eBay pops up every day, but not every program suits every seller. Most companies that put out comprehensive eBay software packages offer options like listing uploading, image hosting, budgeting, and order tracking. Some programs specialize in a few areas, while others go above and beyond with market research support and programs for running larger operations on eBay.

Depending on the kinds of auctions you want to run, there may be a product out there that is perfect for you. Or you may decide to go with a combination of programs to meet your different needs. If you're planning on using multiple tools, be sure to check that they're compatible with one another. Your best bet may be to find a single, comprehensive tool that does it all. Whatever service you choose, make sure its cost translates into real time savings for you. There's no point switching if the only difference it makes is less money for you. Here are some off-eBay tools -

a. Auctiva

Auctiva is a reliable, helpful tool. It started as a free service and still offers some free tools. But now it offers two flat-rate plans: $2.95 per month for up to 15 listings, and $9.95 per month for unlimited listings. Auctiva has earned rave reviews from eBay sellers for services including listing templates, image hosting, advanced editing features, sales tools, a store, checkout, and more.

b. Auction Hawk

Auction Hawk is a member of the eBay Developers Program and offers several service bundles for auction management at a range of price and function levels. It includes image hosting, listing management, and sales automation tools. Auction Hawk Basic is great for eBay beginners, starting at $12.99 per month for a package that will automate up to 220 auction listings. If you want to grow your eBay business further, though, try the Power level (440 listings for $21.99), the Professional level (880 listings for $29.99), or the Unlimited level, suitable for PowerSellers ($44.99 per month).

c. Zoovy

Zoovy Auction software was specifically designed to meet the needs of eBay sellers. It offers tools for automating and managing image hosting, auction listing, checkout, and order fulfillment, prices vary depending on the features you choose and the size of your eBay business.

d. Vendio

Vendio is the largest third-party supplier of seller services on eBay. Vendio provides a complete range of auction management tools through its Sales Manager and Online Stores products, including listing creation, shopping carts, and shipping tools. Costs for services range depending how you choose to pay, a combination of listing fees, monthly rates, and final value fees. You can also pay at a variable rate for different combinations of services. Vendio recommends different levels of service according to your eBay selling volume.

When you're trying to choose the auction software that's best for you, take some time to walk carefully through each tool's product features and specifications in order to choose the company that best meets the needs of your business. While most of the products have some features in common, you might discover that one meets your needs more effectively than another. You can also make use of the eBay Solutions Finder to find the right tool for the job. Taking your eBay business outside eBay can be well worth the effort. eBay wants sellers to succeed, and offers dozens of useful time-saving tools, but sometimes the third-party developers come up with really innovative ideas and just try harder. If you've looked at your business and found a need, then check it out in the Solutions Directory and give it a try. Don't forget to post your review and let others know how it helped you.

Chapter Four

eBay Marketing Strategies

1. Your About Me Page

A. Build trust

You've probably seen these little blue and red me tags beside some eBay user IDs. When you click a seller's me, you can view that person's About Me page. About Me is where you tell the eBay community more about yourself. It's an excellent opportunity to establish your credibility as a seller and build relationships with your potential customers. This page is an underused and powerful tool for eBay sellers. Think of this page as a mini-website for marketing your business. If you're serious about making your eBay business profitable, you can't ignore this valuable piece of eBay real estate. As a seller, you want potential customers to trust you. Your About Me page can showcase information that makes your customers comfortable with you.

a. Write a short biography

Tell potential customers a little bit about who you are and where you're from. Keep it friendly and light in tone, but not overly personal. Include details like your participation in professional organizations and the length of time you have devoted to becoming an expert in your field. The real purpose here is to show why you are a reliable person to buy from.

b. Show your eBay history

Tell people about the things you sell and how you got started. Share your experience and background as an eBay buyer. Even if you're making your first sales, don't let that stop you from including a "business bio." You can talk about the off-eBay experience you bring to your role as an eBay seller.

c. Include relevant information

This kind of information shows your buyers that you know your business and that you are willing to share your knowledge.

d. Anticipate questions and include a FAQ

By including a Frequently Asked Questions section on your About Me page, you can anticipate your buyer's questions and answer them up front. If buyers get the answers they need from you, they will be more inclined to buy from you instead of a competitor who appears less informed or less helpful.

e. Show off your feedback

Feedback is a powerful tool for buyers who are considering whether or not to bid on a seller's items. By including your Feedback on your About Me page, you are showing potential customers you have feedback you're proud to share and you value what your customers say about you.

f. Include terms and conditions

Adding your terms and conditions to your About Me page can clear up questions potential bidders may have. When adding this information, keep this in mind, don't include information that is different or more detailed than the terms of sale you provide on your auction listing pages and be polite.

Your About Me page gives you the opportunity to treat your potential buyers with respect and share helpful information. This will make them more likely to view you as a trustworthy seller and one they would like to buy from.

B. <u>Direct traffic with your about me page</u>

Your About Me page is the only page where eBay allows you to include a link to a page off eBay. eBay is in business to make money, and every customer who clicks away from their site is far less likely to return and bid on something than a customer who never left the eBay site in the first place. That's why eBay restricts where and when you can include links that lead away from their site. As long as you're careful to follow a few guidelines, you can maximize the value of this link while still following eBay's policies.

a. Where you can't send people

Before adding a link to your About Me page, there are two policy restrictions you should know. If you break these restrictions, eBay will penalize you -

- Links to competing websites
- Off-eBay sales pages

b. Where you can send people

- Your active auctions on eBay
- Your eBay Store
- Your website (carefully!)

When linking from your About Me page to your website, take care that the items you offer for sale on your own site are not in conflict with eBay's regulations. If you're offering any items for sale on your website that are also available in your eBay listings, make sure you are not offering a lower price on your site, as this violates eBay's policies. There are restrictions on how you can link to your website, there is no question at all that you should link to it. The benefits to you are enormous. Before creating a link to your website, make sure you check the most recent policy updates about what is and is not allowed.

C. <u>Formatting your About Me page</u>

Building a great About Me page that promotes different aspects of your business is a lot easier than building a website. Before you create your About Me page, take some time to look at the ones that other sellers have made. You'll see a wide variety of professionalism and overall quality, some of them will be great models for your own page, and some of them won't. All of them tell you something about the seller's personality and interests but not all of them do a good job of building customer relationships or of convincing potential customers that the seller is trustworthy.

Finding an example of a really great About Me page isn't as easy as it sounds for some reason most eBay sellers just don't capitalize on the possibilities this page presents. If you pay attention to the bad AboutMe pages, you'll see that they lack the critical elements of design and content. This results in an About Me page that hints at a lack of professionalism and that makes buyers nervous. Good About Me pages have a design that's clean, professional-looking, appealing, and easy to read. And they use that design to share information that builds a professional image and promotes sales.

When you start setting up your About Me page, eBay asks if you want to use their step-by-step process or create your own HTML. Following eBay's step-by-step process is a good choice for sellers with little HTML experience because you don't have to worry about page layout issues like page width or columns. A little HTML knowledge goes a long way to giving your page a spark of individuality and interest. Even if you follow eBay's automated process, you'll see that you have the option of using some of your own HTML in the text fields. We'll talk more about HTML later.

a. Customize your content

To start creating your About Me page, click the Create About Me at this page http://pages.ebay.com/help/account/about-me.html. The step-by-step page has five fields you can begin customizing right away.

a. Title

This is your headline. You want to attract people's attention and make them want to keep reading. It should contain keywords so it attracts the right attention from Search Engines, as well as the attention of targeted buyers.

b. Paragraphs

Even though the form has only two text fields for paragraphs, you're not limited to two paragraphs of total content. Within each of the two paragraph text fields, you can use HTML <p> tags to create as many paragraphs as you want. If you don't use <p> tags in the text fields, everything in one field will display as one paragraph. As with your title, use keywords in the paragraph fields to make your content come up when people search.

c. Images

It is possible to add more images by using HTML image tags in your paragraph text fields if you host the files yourself or use an image hosting service. You don't have a lot of control over your final page layout, and adding extra images, especially if they are of different sizes and shapes.

The most important part of your About Me page is the content you put in the title and paragraph fields. If you do nothing else, make sure you spend time making this information as useful, interesting, and relevant as possible. Don't forget to proofread carefully, nothing devalues your message faster than careless typos or bad grammar. Your My World page is another great way to attract potential customers from off eBay. My World features search tags that other eBayers can use to find you. Better yet, Google, Yahoo, and the other search engines look for these tags.

b. Show off Feedback, listings, and links

You can publish your About Me page as-is but it is recommended that you also include links to display your Feedback your auction listings, and even an off-eBay link -

- Feedback - This section gives you a great chance to build your credibility with your potential buyers. If your Feedback is excellent, then of course you will want to display five to 10 comments on your About Me page.
- Current listings - You should always display the maximum number of current listings allowed on your About Me page. Your buyers will see other items that might interest them, and the listings give them an easy way to navigate to your auctions.
- Links - Your About Me page is the only place on eBay where you can link to an off-eBay website.

Remember, you have a lot more freedom on your own website than you have anywhere on eBay. If you don't already have your own website, put this on your to-do list for when you've got your eBay business up and running. After you complete the first page of the step-by-step process, you can choose from one of three page layout designs and preview your page before submitting it. If you don't like what you see, don't worry, you can always use the Back button. Whenever you look at your own About Me page, you'll see an Edit link that's only available to you and will allow you to make changes.

c. Use HTML to add professional formatting

HTML is the programming language used to create websites. Although you don't need to learn it inside out to be able to run eBay auctions, you can use it to add some professional formatting details to your About Me page. All it takes is a few lines of code that you can copy and paste into your product descriptions. It really is easy. You can use a free HTML editor like Blue Voda to create formatted copy. HTML uses what are known as "tags." Tags come in pairs, an opening tag and a closing tag. These tags are "wrapped" around words to indicate how they should be displayed. Several areas of your product description can be made to look much better through HTML tags -

a. Create an eye-catching headline

Make your headline text bigger than the rest of your description - There's no use in writing a great headline and then hiding it away. You can make the type larger than the rest of the text by adding <h1> tags before and after your headline -

<h1>My Headline</h1>

b. Use bold and italics

Traditional typography uses **bold** and *italics* to emphasize words. In HTML the principle is the same, but bold uses <strong> tags, and italics uses <em>. Here's how they look -

<strong>Bold is strong</strong>, <em>Italic is em</em>

c. Get more than 2 paragraphs of text

You can create a new paragraph in HTML any time, all you have to do is wrap a couple of paragraph tags around a block of text. You can even create paragraphs within that block of text -

<p>This is my item description paragraph. It all has to fit into a single text field, but I want more than one paragraph.</p><p>Good thing I can create more using these simple paragraph tags!</p>

Any text that is wrapped in paragraph tags will appear as a neat block of text with blank lines before and after it.

d. Add lists

Lists are fast and easy to read, and pretty easy to code in html. You can go with a bulleted list or numbers –

<p>Bulleted (or "unordered") list of benefits:</p>
<ul>
<li>benefit 1</li>
<li>benefit 2</li>
<li>benefit 3</li>
</ul>

Or

<p>Numbered (or "ordered") list of benefits:</p>
<ol>
<li>benefit 1</li>
<li>benefit 2</li>
<li>benefit 3</li>
</ol>

e. Link to other web pages

Creating links is what HTML was invented for. A link is made up of two components: The text that users actually click, and the URL of the web page where you'll be sending them. One might look like this -

<p><a href="http://www.yoursite.com">Click here for information about my newsletter</a>. Featuring interviews with parrot training experts!</p>

f. eBay-specific HTML tags

eBay has created some special eBay-only HTML tags that you can use. These are special tags that won't work on sites outside of eBay because they show information specific to eBay, like your listings, your Feedback, and your eBay User ID. If you're an HTML newbie you might want to wait until you have a handle on the basic tags before you get into these special ones.

D. Collecting opt-ins

Have you ever subscribed to an email newsletter? If so, you belong to an opt-in email list, a list of people who have given a specific person or company permission to contact them by email. As a business owner, you want to send legitimate opt-in email, not spam. That means you need to begin building a list of people who have given you permission to contact them. This way, if you promote your products by email, you'll know your messages are only going to people who want them. It is within eBay's rules to use what's called an opt-in form on your About Me page to collect your potential customers' email addresses. Few eBay sellers use an opt-in form and if you don't, you're turning down the chance to build a growing opt-in subscriber list.

An opt-in list allows you to develop relationships of trust and respect with people who want to hear from you. They have elected to receive messages from you, so that tells you they already believe in you and your products. They're your best potential customers. An opt-in list allows you to market to these customers again and again by email for free. You can send them news items related to the products you sell, updates about your business, news about new deals you're offering and more. This gives you opportunities for generating repeat business that you wouldn't have otherwise. Your opt-in form needs to give your visitors a compelling offer to attract their interest. Give them a reason to sign up, one that is targeted to their interests and watch your customer list grow. One reason customers subscribe is to receive a free newsletter. There are many other enticing offers you can put on your About Me page. You could offer a free eBook, article, screensaver, patterns, plans, or games they can download, or let them take part in a survey, poll, or contest to win a prize. Consider what it is that will keep your customers coming back and be creative in what you offer them. They'll come back again and again, giving you plenty of opportunities for repeat business and backend sales. Make sure that every time you create an auction listing, you include a link to your About Me page and encourage users to sign up for your opt-in offer. You could say Visit my About Me page to receive a free newsletter and find out about this month's discounts.

E. <u>Tune-up</u>

The true test of your About Me page is the effect it will have when a visitor arrives to review it. To get an idea of how your About Me page looks to your visitors, open it in your web browser and check it against these points.

- The 10-second scan test, read the content of your page. Look at the headline, sub headlines, the highlighted and the emphasized text. Will visitors get a good idea of who you are and what you are selling?
- Is the content relevant?
- Does it make customers feel comfortable with the seller?
- Are there keywords in your headlines and page content?
- Does it highlight your relevant expertise or experience?
- Does the page include a high-quality logo and photo?
- Does the page include Feedback comments?
- Does the page include payment information and a good guarantee?
- Was the page customized using HTML?
- Does it include an FAQ section?
- Does the page have an opt-in email form?
- Are there links to your eBay Store and existing auctions?
- Does it showcase your best items?
- Is it positive and friendly?
- Does the page include one or more calls to action?

Now that you know how to analyze your About Me page, your first priority is to apply these steps to your about me page. It's easy for buyers to miss seeing the tiny me image link beside your user ID, so you should promote your About Me page directly on every auction you list. If you use a template to create new auctions, create a link directly in that template that generates interest in what is on your About Me page and encourage viewers to click on it. Make sure your About Me page links back to your auctions so visitors can bid. After reading your About Me page, your buyers should feel even more confident about bidding on your auctions, so give them an easy route back with a list of links to all your active auctions.

2. Attract Internet Traffic

A. <u>Optimize listings for search engines</u>

Sometimes, selling things on eBay is as simple as putting up a listing and watching the bids roll in. But it's not always that easy. The key to creating bidding is traffic and lots of it. You've learned how to attract the attention of eBayers both those who search by keywords and those who will drill down through categories. Now it's time to pull in people who are surfing on Google or Yahoo. People who type one or more keywords into a search engine such as Google have already focused their attention on a particular product or category. They are targeted customers who have a good idea of what they want.

Among the results they get after typing their terms into a search engine, one of your eBay listings may show up but unless you've designed your listings to do that, it's unlikely to happen on its own. There are a number of ways to get noticed by potential customers who are searching for items like yours off-eBay.

a. Create your off-eBay website

Creating your own website and making it attract the big search engines is an effective way to drive traffic to your eBay auctions. The site doesn't have to be large or complex, a straightforward website designed with only HTML is more easily found and indexed by search engines than sites with intricate design and complicated technology. There are three things you must do to optimize your website for search engines -

a. Write high-quality content

The quality of the content on your web pages largely determines the attention you get from search engines. But creating content that uses keywords for the sole purpose of getting high search results, instead of for providing useful information, is called keyword spamming and it's not a good plan. You'll have better results if you develop your page content to avoid keyword spamming. Providing relevant content is one of the most important strategies to optimize your website.

b. Acquire inbound links

Inbound links are links that bring a visitor from another website directly to yours. There are two types of inbound links: reciprocal and non-reciprocal. A non-reciprocal link is when someone links to your website from theirs, without you linking back. These are what the search engines look for. You can get non-reciprocal links by writing articles about something related to your products and distributing them on the Internet's free article directories.

c. The code behind your website

Each one of your website pages has its own meta data, information about the site itself that is used by the search engines. This information is contained in HTML tags in your code that tell the search engines how to index your page and to display the results when someone does a search for terms you've used. The Title tag is one of the most important for helping search engines find your site easily. It contains the text that appears at the very top of the browser page. Search engines love the words in the title tag, so don't waste them. Put your most important keywords in your title to maximize their appeal to search engines.

Make sure that you have a unique title tag for each page on your site. A unique tag will help identify the purpose or contents of the page not only for search engines, but also for visitors navigating your site. Other types of code worth mentioning are the tags for Keywords and Description. Like the title tag, these tags should be custom written for each page on your site. If you make the description tags for each page unique, your site will attract more highly targeted traffic than if you use the same generic meta data for every page. Another great place to add a few keywords is in the alt text of any images you have. The alt text of images is used by Google Image Search to index images. It's also displayed on a webpage if the images can't be displayed for some reason. Make sure that each page on your website encourages the visitor to click through to your eBay auction listings. Remember, your main purpose in creating this site is to give your auction listings more visibility outside eBay than they can get on their own.

b. Drive traffic to your eBay Store

Items in eBay Stores are more likely than regular auction listings to attract the attention of external search engines. The techniques we discussed in the previous section for helping search engines find your website apply equally to the creation of your eBay Store. You want to make sure that you have high-quality content, that you obtain as many relevant links to your Store as you can, and that you use your HTML meta tags to define and label the content of each page. Remember eBay limits how you can link away from your Store. Make sure you don't link directly to pages that link anywhere else.

eBay provides you with an export listings link that third parties can use to download a current list of your inventory. Many shopping malls and directories will accept this file format to list the items for sale in your eBay Store. According to the Google Base help, you don't need to submit your store listings to Google, eBay submits listings directly to Google on a regular basis. Another great way to drive traffic to your store is to get relevant links from directories and relevant sites. You'll want to ensure that you have updated your store search engine keywords to create search phrases that your potential customers are currently using.

c. Use keywords on your About Me and My World pages

Think of your About Me page as the home page to your website and you'll see how the web page optimization principles we discussed earlier also apply to your About Me page. While you can't control the meta data (title, meta keywords, and meta description) on your About Me page, you do have control over your keywords and content. These things will attract search engine spiders like a magnet, so make sure that you design your About Me page with them in mind. It is entirely possible to get your About Me page to show up on the first or second page of search results if you apply the right optimization strategies.

Take a few minutes to make sure that your About Me page is optimized, and you'll see the results in increased traffic. My World does the same sort of job as your About Me page in that it allows you to tell your store and auction visitors who you are, what you offer, and what your Feedback is. My World doesn't allow you to use HTML to add your own elements. It does offer some interesting features -

- A list of your feedback
- Space to outline your interests
- An extensive bio area
- Search tags where you can enter keywords
- The ability to add a picture of yourself
- A list of your current items for sale
- The ability to tag your MyWorld page with words your target market might be interested in

You can set up your own MyWorld page and use it along with your About Me page to increase your visibility in the search engines.

B. Targeted traffic to your store

One of the main attractions of operating an eBay Store is that the listing fees cost pennies. Unfortunately, the Final Value Fees are higher than the ones you'd pay if the same item sold for the same price in an Auction style listing. One way you can save money on your fees is by bringing traffic to eBay from an outside site or link. There are several ways that you can set this up, and all of them give you a Store Referral Credit, cutting 75% off your Final Value Fees. In order to qualify your sale for the Store Referral Credit, you'll need to get a buyer to either click a link containing your referral code or type your eBay Store's URL into the address bar of their web browser.

A buyer who takes either of these two actions will land on one of your Store's pages. They must then purchase one of your eBay Store items during that shopping session for eBay to register your fee credit. Your best bet for attracting this kind of money-saving traffic to your eBay Store is to place your links in front of as many potential buyers as possible and to make sure that each of those links contains your referral code. To create your referral code, add this piece of code to the end of your Store URL -

?refid=store

For the best visibility, place links containing your referral code in -

- Your email signature line
- Any inbound link from another website
- Your pay-per-click advertising

Pay-per-click (PPC) advertising, in particular, is a great place to make use of this code. That's because any purchases made by buyers can help offset your PPC advertising costs. In addition, PPC advertising has the potential of reaching a much wider audience than your own email or newsletters ever could. Google's AdWords and Yahoo's Sponsored Search are the two best ways to start your PPC ad campaign. These two pay-per-click search engines will place your ads in front of thousands more targeted buyers than you could hope to reach alone. With both the Google and the Yahoo paid ad programs, you bid on keywords, establishing the maximum you'll pay per click and per day, your ads are then displayed on search results pages associated with those keywords.

C. __Promotion strategies__

There are other strategies for getting traffic from outside eBay to your eBay listings. They are not necessarily as effective as the ones we've discussed but they are worth testing to see if they work to make your items more visible to buyers.

a. Create a consistent, professional image

When you start selling on eBay, you need to start thinking of yourself and your eBay Store as a company or small corporation. Like any company, you have to create a consistent image. Repetition and consistency make your eBay presence memorable. One way to create a consistent eBay image is to put your User ID or your eBay Store name on any material that anyone outside your business will come in contact with. This means that all packaging, including boxes, wrapping paper, and ribbon, should always be consistent. In addition to your User ID or eBay Store name, include your contact information and a short blurb about your products as prominently as possible. Prepare inserts for your packages, such as business cards, flyers, brochures, and other promotional materials. Some eBay sellers use these materials to offer customers discounts on the price or shipping of their next purchase to encourage repeat business.

b. Use a blog to drive traffic

A blog is a great way to attract attention for your eBay items. It's an online journal or website that has regular, frequent updates and additions to its content, and is organized by date of entry with the most recent article first. There are some advantages to using a blog to promote your eBay business -

- You can write articles that are full of keywords related to your products
- You can generate a lot more inbound links than you can on eBay
- You can attract traffic from search engines
- You can establish your credibility and create a sense of community
- You can actively drive your viewers to your auctions or eBay Store
- You can showcase your auctions
- You have a lot of freedom with images

c. Make yourself known in forums and discussion groups

Buyers appreciate knowing that the person they are sending money to really knows their business. By establishing yourself as an expert or a reliable source of information, you build credibility for yourself as a seller. One easy way to share your expertise and experience is to participate in online forums and discussion groups. eBay's own discussion boards are a good starting point for this. Find a category or topic that interests you, follow the discussion for a while to get a sense of the flow and protocol, and start answering questions or offering advice. There are plenty of other eBay-related boards, forums, and groups that take place off-eBay.

d. Publish articles in your area of expertise

Becoming known as an expert goes beyond your participation in online forums. To really establish yourself write articles for other people's websites. Website owners are always looking for relevant content to beef up their sites. Offer your articles to them for free, with the understanding that they will provide a link to your website, eBay Store, or About Me page. Readers will see that your articles have been endorsed by a site they already trust, so they will trust you by association. That will make them much more inclined to click on your link than they otherwise would.

The key to getting this traffic is to write articles that are truly useful and interesting to the readers. Other website owners won't be interested in your writing if it doesn't provide information that enhances the reputation and value of their own site. Remember to always include a link to your site or eBay Store in an About the Author blurb at the end of your article.

e. eBay Reviews & Guides

One great place that combines the benefits of discussion boards and article publishing is eBay's Reviews & Guides. Although writing reviews can be helpful, especially in increasing your reviewer rank, guides are more effective for SEO and increasing traffic for keyword-specific items. When writing a guide or a review, you need to focus on putting keywords in your title, body text, and tags because they're what drive search engine traffic. You can also upload pictures, which give you another opportunity to insert keywords, in the image filename and alt text. Another aspect to consider is the Reviewer Rank. This appears to be based on a combination of total positive votes and helpfulness. The more useful and content-rich your guide is, the better it'll be at attracting positive votes.

Getting relevant reviews and guides found by people searching on Google will increase traffic to your store, listings, and About Me page. Ideally, you should write guides related to the products you're selling and include a mix of useful information and a light pitch for your products. You can include keyword-rich links in your guides but they have to be eBay links. You should always include links to your store, your About Me page, and a link to all your listings.

f. Google base

Google is the world's number one search engine. What you may or may not know is that Google has spent the last few years developing and acquiring a suite of online services that make it into more than just a place to search. One of these services, called Google Base, lets you submit information about anything you'd like people to be able to find online. It wasn't originally developed as an online marketplace but it evolved into one.

It only takes a few seconds to create an account on Google Base, and if your business is 100% eBay-based, you don't have to worry about submitting your listings to it they'll show up. Because the service is thoroughly integrated with Google Search, you'll be increasing the exposure your products receive in Google's search results. Remember that store referral code you learned about earlier. Google lets you include a URL in your product listing on Google Base, by including a direct link to your eBay Store for each product, along with your referral code, you'll save 75% on your listings and get greater exposure in the search results.

3. Be an Active Member of the eBay Community

A. <u>Strategize eBay sellers</u>

Social networking and Web 2.0 might sound like a couple of overused buzzwords but don't let that blind you to the opportunities that exist in social networking for maximizing your eBay success. Social networking websites allow groups of users to gather, network, and exchange information on their shared interests. These kinds of sites are widely believed to represent the future of the Internet bringing people together. In the last couple of years we've seen their popularity explode, with sites like YouTube, MySpace, and Facebook attracting millions of new users. eBay itself has a very active community of users and if you join and participate in that community you can drive even more buyers to your auctions.

If you operate a part-time business out of your living room, it can be tempting to sit behind the computer screen and keep interaction with other sellers to a bare minimum. But networking is the cornerstone of many successful businesses and eBay is no exception. Many successful eBayers credit the feedback, tips, and tricks they've learned from other eBay sellers as key to ramping up their eBay auction sales. eBay's chat rooms and seller groups provide a great opportunity to network with like-minded sellers. Whether you're just starting out or hoping to expand your already successful business, there's always room to learn and grow.

One hot spot is eBay Groups, where you can join a special-interest group and participate in discussions, or create your own group complete with a shared photo album and newsletter. It's also worth checking out these community message boards, similar to eBay Groups -

- eBay Discussion Groups - Get help on specific topics, categories, workshops, and more
- eBay Chat Rooms - Chat about categories and eBay, ask questions, or just talk

These sites are great places to connect with other buyers and sellers and chat about all things eBay. You can get feedback on your business, or even just read what others have to say. And that kind of information is invaluable when it comes to uncovering new business strategies you may not have thought of yourself. Your closest competitors may be taking part in the discussions on these sites, so you'll want to be careful about how many of your own strategies you reveal.

B. Social network tools

eBay has always encouraged a sense of community on its site through its message boards and feedback system, as well as a whole raft of features that make it easier than ever for users to interact in new ways.

- Skype - Skype is a voice-over-IP (VOIP) system that acts like a phone on the Internet. eBay purchased Skype in 2005 and has been steadily integrating it into its own site so buyers and sellers can use it to communicate easily with one another. Skype is free to use, and as an eBay seller, you can add easy voice and chat links to your listings that let potential buyers get in touch instantly and ask questions.
- MyCollectibles – This is hosted on Kaboodle, a partner site of eBay. It's a place for collectors to showcase their collectibles, meet others with similar interests, and discuss their collections.
- My World – Every eBay user is assigned a My World page, which is a more social-minded version of the About Me page. Users can add a profile that shares their interests, hobbies, business information, and more.
- eBay Neighborhoods - Connect with other people who share your interests and loves.

The one worth spending some time developing is My World. My World pages tend to get a good page rank in Google, so yours has a terrific chance of turning up high in Google's search results. The My World hub features a list of tags, which are labels that people use to describe their interests. When you click a tag, you'll see a list of other people who use those labels, so this is a great tool for both finding and attracting other eBayers who share your interests. The Listing tags are especially good for driving potential customers from search engines. Visit the hub and note all the tags being used that describe your products and areas of expertise, then add those tags to your own My World page so like-minded buyers and sellers can find you.

If meeting online doesn't do it for you, go one step further and consider meeting up with eBay Sellers in your area. Meetup is a site that connects people with a particular interest to other locals who are interested in the same things. There are almost 5,000 eBayers on Meetup and they're actively getting together to brainstorm new ways to ramp up their eBay earnings and reach untapped pockets of potential customers. This service is free to join and allows you to search for eBay meetings in your area by topic or by city. You can start your own eBay Seller Group, and Meetup will automatically email other sellers in your area who have also listed eBay as one of their interests. For more on eBay Meetup groups, check the special section of their site devoted to eBayers.

Chapter Five

Expand Your Business

1. Create loyal bidders

A. <u>Get on Favorite Sellers lists</u>

The Favorite Sellers list allows every eBay member to add their favorite sellers to a list contained within their My eBay area. This bookmarks those seller's profiles, much as you would save a favorite website in your Internet browser, so eBay members can quickly find the current auctions of their preferred sellers. Here are a few reasons why you should work hard to get customers to add you to their Favorite Sellers list -

- Buyers can return to your auctions easily because your items are saved in their My eBay
- You can email your Top Picks through eBay to anyone who has added you to their list
- Send a regular newsletter to subscribers if you have an eBay store to keep in touch

Each auction listing you create will automatically display an Add to Favorite Sellers link under the Meet the seller box at the top, so make sure you take advantage of this opportunity to collect loyal subscribers. All you have to do is add a line or two of text to your listing, reminding people to click the link so they can learn more about you and the items you're selling. The benefits you gain from being added to buyers' Favorite Sellers lists are too good to be missed, yet many eBay sellers don't push their buyers toward this feature. If you do, you'll be able to keep your auctions in front of your target audience long after they've visited your listings.

B. Create a RSS feed

RSS is an increasingly popular way for Internet users to get new content and updates from all kinds of websites instantly sent to one convenient location. RSS feeds fresh content in real time to anyone who requests it. All it takes is an RSS reader, and there are dozens of great, free RSS readers available, including NewsGator, Bloglines, My Yahoo, My MSN, and Google Reader, among many others. The latest versions of most web browsers, including Internet Explorer and Firefox, can read and save RSS feed links as well.

eBay RSS feeds offer news announcements and discussion boards, have some great features that allow sellers to benefit more from RSS. Any time eBay posts a new announcement, it will automatically show up in your RSS feed reader. The little orange box is labeled XML because that's the language you write an RSS feed in. XML looks a lot like HTML.

a. Notify your customers instantly when you have new products

eBay shoppers can now get instant updates from their favorite eBay Stores using RSS. If you have a store, this means that any buyer who clicks your RSS button will get immediate notice of any new items posted for sale in your store. It's a great way to keep satisfied customers coming back for more. If you've been running a professional eBay business with great Feedback, you've already built a trusting business relationship with your clients. Using RSS, you can now tell everyone about your newest items the moment they are available. It only takes a couple of clicks for store owners to turn on the basic RSS feed for their store.

b. Capture a bigger audience for in-demand items

Not only can your customers get instant updates on your store items, they can also now sign up RSS feeds on specific search items. A user looking for a hard-to-find item will be notified as soon as someone lists the item for sale. This saves the customer from having to search for it every day. Buyers simply run their search, narrow down their options to include exactly what they're looking for, then copy the RSS link into their RSS feed reader. If you list rare, collectible, and hard-to-find items in categories that are in demand, you can now be assured that serious collectors will be more likely to find what they're hunting for.

C. Start an email relationship with bidders

Email is one of the most effective and profitable tools you have at your disposal to promote your auctions and build your eBay business. You can email customers and subscribers to notify them of your latest auctions. Email marketing is fast, effective, personal and free. No matter what business you are in, no matter what you sell, you can increase your profits using email marketing. Getting started with email marketing can seriously increase the profits you generate through your eBay business. Very few sellers know how to use email marketing effectively.

Your opt-in email list is made up of people who want to hear from you. You're giving them something they've asked you for. When someone signs up to receive email from you and find out about your auctions, they understand that you'll be sending them information they actually want to receive, meaning that your opt-in list will be highly responsive to your email promotions. Email allows you to contact the people on your list over and over again, so you can build valuable lifetime relationships with them.

a. eBay's email tools

eBay has an email forwarding system you can use to upsell, cross-promote, and push your customers back to your other auctions or eBay store. It's not a perfect system, as the relationship being maintained is really between eBay and your customer. A completely personal-looking email coming directly from you can have a far more powerful effect. Despite these minor drawbacks, there are ways that you can maximize the usefulness of communications with your customers -

- Customize your eBay invoices
- Customize your PayPal emails

As you know eBay automatically sends end-of-auction emails that notify winning bidders that they need to pay you for their item. You can customize the content of these emails by adding your own message, or you can use autotext to personalize the message by including details like the Buyer's User ID. This is a good opportunity to direct customers to your other listings or to ask them to make you a Favorite Seller. If you have an eBay Store, your options are greater. You can create your own email newsletter and send it to up to 4,000 people, depending on your level of store, who subscribe through the Add to Favorite Sellers link in your auctions.

eBay provides templates for you to use when setting up this newsletter and you can-

- Include your store logo at the top of your newsletter
- Write your own newsletter content
- Choose which of your store listings you want to feature
- Feature individual auctions that you're currently running

The great thing about these emails is that your recipients can click through to your auctions directly from their email. eBay lets you track how many click-throughs you get so you can analyze your success. If you have an eBay Store, this is a feature well worth testing to see how many more bids and sales you can generate through it. Even if you don't have an eBay Store, you can still use email marketing to communicate with your bidders and customers. The alternative to using eBay's email system is to collect the email addresses of your customers and auction visitors and establish a relationship directly with them, with the aim of funneling them back to your auctions to buy from you again, as well as offering them more products related to their original purchases.

b. Collect opt-ins yourself

When people sign up to receive your electronic messages, they are opting in to your mail list. Because they have requested information from you, your messages are not considered to be junk mail, spam, or unsolicited email. Sending messages and information to people who have given you permission to contact them is the best way to build the kind of relationships that will encourage a steady flow of traffic. There are three ways you can maximize your opportunities to keep in touch with your bidders and customers and sell them more items.

- Make use of your existing opt-in list
- Collect opt-in email addresses from your About Me page
- Collect opt-ins on your own website

Before you start marketing your eBay listings by email, it's important to understand the restrictions eBay places on the way sellers can conduct business. eBay discourages any techniques that lead to an eBay seller doing business with a buyer off eBay. This means sellers are not allowed to direct eBay shoppers to a web page that sells the same items they have listed on eBay. eBay makes its money from its auction listing and final selling fees, so any attempts to bypass these fees are frowned upon and can lead to eBay canceling your auctions or even suspending your account.

You can use an email management service to easily manage these valuable contacts and build long-term relationships that let you sell to them again, without turning answering your email into a full-time job.

D. Email marketing strategies

Email marketing is powerful because it lets you get more value out of each customer you acquire by marketing more products to them. There are two strategies you'll need to use for great results.

a. Sell backend products

A backend product is a product you sell to a customer after they've made a purchase. It should be something closely related to the original purpose. Backend products can add extra dollars to each sale you make through eBay with very little effort on your part. In fact, 30% to 50% of your customers who were satisfied with their original purchase will buy from you again if you offer them a related product. There are all kinds of backend products you can sell but one good strategy is to create and sell an information product. The advantage of this strategy is that information products are cheap and easy to produce, and can be delivered on CD along with the item you're sending to the buyer.

b. Writing powerful email promotions

Now that you know the ways to take advantage of the positive relationships you've built, you need to put them to work for you. Don't get overwhelmed by the details. Just remember that writing email promotions is all about following a formula -

- Choose your offer
- Focus on benefits, not features
- A strong opening paragraph
- Focus on the customer
- Create urgency
- Include your contact information
- Include a call to action
- Add "unsubscribe" instructions

Once you've run through these steps, give your promotion the 10-second scan test and make sure it passes. The secret to writing email promotions that drive people to your listings is to follow the instructions we've given you and practice. Challenge yourself to spend just one hour writing an email promotion while reviewing the techniques we've given. The first one you write might seem a bit difficult, since you'll be getting used to writing. Once you get comfortable with the process, it should only take you 20 or 30 minutes to write a promotion.

E. Automate your email

When you create a mailing list of email addresses, you're taking a leap beyond all your competitors. Email marketing is one of the most powerful and inexpensive ways for online businesses to market their products and services. The best part is you can use an email marketing service to put most of your email chores on autopilot. Using an email service provider you can automatically take care of tasks.

a. Manage subscribe requests

Keeping on top of your subscribe requests is a critical process that helps ensure each and every mailing you send is optimized to guarantee maximum profits. If someone takes the time to give you their email address, then it's reasonable to assume that this person is interested in your product or service. If you don't take the time to add their address to your list in time for your next mailing, you're losing money. The good news is that you don't have to copy and paste each new email address into your mailing list. Your email service will automate the job of adding new subscribers to your list and will check for duplicate subscribers.

b. Manage unsubscribe requests

Managing unsubscribe requests is the most important part of list management. Sometimes people decide they don't want to receive emails from you anymore and ask to be unsubscribed. If you don't unsubscribe them, any further email you send them is spam, which can have serious consequences. An advantage to using an email management service is that it will automatically delete people from your list as soon as they ask to be unsubscribed.

c. Send out autoresponders

These are messages that go out automatically in response to certain events, for instance a Thank you for purchasing email. You use a standard template for each message and it can be customized for the individual receiving it. Selling Manager Pro has automation to let buyers know when they've won an item and helpfully adds a link to your other listings. In the your item has been shipped notification email, there is a link that enables a buyer to add you to their list of favorite sellers with just one click.

d. Personalize each message

In addition to automatically subscribing and unsubscribing new contacts, email service providers make the task of merging and sending personalized email messages very easy. It will merge the first name of the recipient into the Subject line of the email.

F. Make opt-ins eager

Once you have your list set up and automated, you can concentrate on what you are sending your valued eBay customers and subscribers, the content of your emails.

They have subscribed for a reason. You made them promises, now it is time to follow through.

- Send a sign-up confirmation
- Develop relationships by offering free information

Once you've captured their email address and established your credibility by offering them valuable information, your chances of these people returning to bid in your auctions increase. That's because you've established a relationship and earned their trust and respect by giving them the information they're looking for. Then you can -

- Announce weekly specials
- Offer discounts
- Send follow-up offers
- Encourage referrals

2. International Markets

A. <u>You're international</u>

The first thing you should do to capture the interest of international buyers is to tell them you're there. Having done that, you can get your products right under their noses using one of these methods -

- Select Worldwide shipping during the listing process
- Create a separate listing on other international eBay sites
- Use the International Site Visibility Listing Upgrade

The International Site Visibility upgrade allows you to list on your local eBay site as well as show up in the default search results on select global eBay sites for less than it would cost to list individually. Considering the low upgrade fee for the International Visibility Listing it's certainly a safe bet even if you just want to test the waters. It gives you more exposure than the "worldwide" shipping option, and it's cheaper and easier than listing on individual sites. You can encourage international bids on your item and avoid having to answer more email by including shipping rates to international destinations on all your listings. Letting your buyers know exactly how much they'll pay for shipping removes the uncertainty that may prevent them from bidding. eBay's International Flat Rate or Calculated Shipping options give you an easy way to include rates in your listing. The free Shipping Calculator provides instant shipping costs to buyers everywhere and a number of big advantages to the sellers who feature it -

- Listings that include the Shipping Calculator are more likely to sell
- Shipping details are pre-filled when your buyer goes to checkout
- eBay will display one total cost to buyers
- You can make multiple shipping services available to your buyers
- Buyers will see shipping costs specific to their location

Some international shipping options include -

- United States Postal Service (USPS)
- UPS
- Other courier services like FedEx and DHL. They can be more expensive, but your buyers might be willing to pay extra for the ability to track packages and get their items delivered overnight.

B. International payments

All sellers want to get paid quickly and securely. International transactions can make some sellers nervous. After all the stories of scams from overseas, some buyers have completely given up on international sales and only sell locally. It's no secret that shady escrow companies and wire transfers are to be avoided but the answer is simple use PayPal. PayPal is pretty much the most secure payment form you can accept. Plus, you can customize your options so that international payments work the way you want them to. If a buyer pays you in US dollars, the funds are automatically deposited in your account. If they pay in a different currency, you'll be given three options -

- Accept the payment and open a new currency balance
- Accept the payment and convert it to your primary currency
- Block the payment

PayPal charges fees in the currency in which the funds were sent. Payments converted to your primary currency will be converted at the going exchange rate. To learn more about receiving money in multiple currencies, see the Multiple Currencies FAQs in PayPal's Help Center. If you ever find yourself worried that a buyer may be fraudulent or trying to cheat you here are a few guidelines -

- Use PayPal only
- Don't end listings early
- Review the buyer's contact information
- Consider using Escrow.com for high-priced items
- Make sure you have received and confirmed payment before you ship

Visit the eBay Security Center for more information about how to protect yourself as a seller.

C. Protect your shipping DSR

DSRs for shipping are universally the most difficult to do well in. That's because you just can't control how fast your package arrives once you hand it off into the postal system. Poor shipping times are even more problematic for sellers sending their items overseas. Although a small window pops up when a buyer purchases from an international seller to remind them that shipping will take longer than usual, you can't rely on your customer to remember this when they rate you on shipping.

You'll never be able to completely counteract the fact that shipping internationally will take more time, but you can remind your customers of this fact before they leave their feedback. Include a small leaflet on your shipping policies with your package. Be very specific about when you ship, how long shipping usually takes, and remind your customer that you have done your very best to make sure you were able to reach the right balance of speed and cost. You can add your email address and ask that buyers leave comments for you if they were unsatisfied with shipping times. eBay's official policy does allow them to reverse negative or neutral Feedback if that Feedback references customs delays or customs fees. To qualify for having this Feedback removed, you must have this text displayed prominently in your listing -

International Buyers -

- Import duties, taxes, and charges are not included in the item price or shipping charges. These charges are the buyer's responsibility.
- Please check with your country's customs office to determine what these additional costs will be prior to bidding/buying.

If you're still having problems with your shipping DSRs, one strategy is to offer a partial refund on shipping costs to your customer and it won't even cost you a penny. In your listing, hike up your S&H by 50 cents more than it will actually cost you. Then, once you have shipped your package, contact the buyer and inform them that postage ended up being less than you expected, so you are refunding them 50 cents. Not only will this inspire better DSRs for shipping, you will also boost your Communication rating.

D. Packages through customs

Customs can be one of the most worrisome and difficult obstacles faced by international sellers. Customs departments charge a confusing number of different duties and taxes, and can be different for every country you sell to. The good news is that you don't have to worry too much about this. If you clearly state in all your auctions that the buyer is responsible for import tariffs, and you label your item properly, you've got nothing to fear. When you declare the value of the item on the customs form, use the auction closing price of the item, not including shipping and handling costs. Don't declare what you originally paid for the item or what you believe it is worth. If you state an amount higher than the final closing price, the buyer may have to overpay duties and taxes in their country.

It's also a good idea to state the condition of the item if it's used or second-hand, be sure to state that and spare your buyer from having to pay extra duty. You should also include a printout of the closed eBay listing in your package. If customs inspectors examine the package, this will verify that the information on the customs declaration form is true. A lot of buyers will ask you to declare the item a gift so they can avoid paying duties and fees. As tempting as it may be to make your buyer happy at no extra cost to you, remember that it's against the law to misrepresent an item in order to avoid customs fees. Sending out too many gifts may get the attention of the IRS, it's not worth it.

3. Taking Your Business off eBay

A. <u>Your own website</u>

Many people start an eBay business as a first step towards a wider goal of running their own independent online business. It's a great idea whatever your goals, the skills and strategies you learn by selling on eBay will serve you well in your next endeavor. Business moves fast, and online business moves even faster, so you need to get the jump on things. Setting up a website isn't as hard as most people think. There are plenty of tools and resources available to walk you through it step by step, and it's worth the effort. An off-eBay site can boost your eBay business -

- Improve your exposure in the search engine listings
- Increase traffic to your eBay Store and auctions
- Attract more people who opt in to your email list
- Drive up your revenues with another stream of income
- Bring in testimonials from happy customers that build your credibility
- Lower your total eBay and PayPal fees

Even if your first off-eBay website is a simple page with basic information about your business, an opt-in form, some keyword-rich content, and a few links to your eBay Store and auctions, it's going to help your eBay business make more money. Setting up a website may seem like a challenge. But with everything you've learned about selling on eBay, it doesn't have to be a struggle. Just start small and take it one step at a time.

Before you do anything, think about what you want your website to do and write out the information it will contain. Do you want something simple? Do you want to set up an e-commerce site with multiple pages selling different products? Do you want it to feature valuable articles that will attract visitors and search engines? Be clear and focused, then you'll be able to choose the appropriate site-building tools. You'll also need your own domain name, such as www.mysite.com, and a web hosting package that gives you some virtual space to store your website. When choosing your domain name, keep it related to your business, and consider using words in the name that reflect your user ID or eBay Store name.

a. Free templates

For a simple one-page website, Google free website templates and choose something that reflects your business.

b. Make your site a blog

If you're nervous about running your own website, a quick and easy way to get started is by creating a blog. Blogs are simple to create and maintain. They can be useful for promoting your eBay business. Google's Blogger makes it easy to create a blog that's easy to update with information about the products and services you offer.

B. <u>Get visitors to your auctions</u>

eBay's listings get great results in searches on Google and other search engines, which helps sellers find off-eBay bidders for auctions. There are number of ways to attract visitors to your eBay pages from across the Internet.

a. Create keyword-rich pages and sites

If you know your best keywords and use them every chance you get, the search engines will rank your material higher. That means people using your keywords to search for what you sell are more likely to find you. If everything you put on the eBay site links back to your listings, your store, or your About Me page, you'll be on the first page of Google results and ahead of your competition. Use the same strategy on your own website. Look carefully at the keywords people are using to discover your eBay listings, then add keyword-rich content to your site to attract those people when they do searches that use those keywords.

b. Reviews & Guides

You've already read about how writing reviews and guides can help improve your credibility and enhance trust. They also give you another place to be found by the search engines. Feel free to write as long as you want about whatever you want and include as many keyword variations as you can. Every review or guide can link to your About Me page and your My World page, driving more traffic to you and your listings.

c. Affiliate and Internet marketing

You can join eBay's affiliate program and promote anything for sale on eBay, no matter who's selling it, and still make money. Whenever someone clicks your affiliate link to visit eBay, then signs up as an eBay member or purchases any item for sale on eBay, you'll earn a commission. It makes sense to sign up as an eBay affiliate and place a link on your off-eBay site.

d. RSS

Using eBay's RSS feeds, you can run your up-to-the-minute eBay listings on your blog, external website, or other personal homepages. Anyone who clicks on them will be taken directly to the eBay listing. It's a great way to attract more buyers. If you have a store, you'll save 75% on your final value fees for every purchase you've referred. When you're viewing one of your listings, click the List link next to View Seller's Other Items at the right side of the page. This will display a list of the items you're selling, and at the bottom of the search results you'll see the orange RSS icon. This is the RSS feed for a live search for your products. Right-click the icon and select Properties, then copy the full URL.

Next, visit RSSexpress-lite, which is an RSS-to-javascript converter. Paste the URL into the select a channel box and click Get Script. Copy the code they generate, then paste it into the code of your own website or blog. Every time someone loads the page containing the code, they'll see your listings, which are just as current as what you'd see on the eBay site. Use this trick to post feeds of your items to your blog or other site, or do more specific item searches, when you want the items to be more relevant to the content.

e. Shopping sites

The best shopping site to submit your products to is Google Base. There are four reasons -

- It's free
- Google Base is indexed by Google faster than other sites
- Someone can buy your products right on Google Base, without having to visit eBay
- eBay submits listings to Google Base, so you don't have to do anything to have your eBay listings show up there

Google Base can be a great alternative stream of income, and a place where buyers who don't usually visit eBay might just buy what you're selling. Submitting reviews of your products at places like Amazon and other shopping sites is another great way to get links back to your store.

f. Press releases

Sending out a press release can be a great way to get more exposure for your business. The idea is to write a short, informative, entertaining article about some newsworthy event, then submit it to online press release sites and hope it gets published by a major news source. The key is to write something that readers are likely to find interesting. Don't just talk about what products you're offering; share an interesting event or a story about something you've done that will get people interested in learning more about your business.

Once you've written it, do an online search for press release distribution and you'll find several free services that will send out your release. Press releases get picked up on newswires and industry-specific sites and they often appear where sales sites don't. Link the release to your eBay Store and your new site for maximum impact.

4. Advanced Tips and Tricks

A. Create multiple streams of income

Everyone knows that when it comes to auctions, eBay is the best. but there are other auction sites out there too, and they have their own communities of buyers. Sometimes the biggest marketplace out there just isn't your best option, so here are some others for you to check out -

- Half.com - A subsidiary of eBay that specializes in books, music, movies, and video games. If that's your market, and you think you can be competitive, take a look and try listing your items.
- Overstock.com - The second-largest auction site, Overstock Auctions is usually picked as the first non-eBay option. With dozens of categories and several hundred thousand listings, it's probably the most complete auction site this outside of eBay.
- Amazon Marketplace - Amazon is its own mini-empire there are tons of people out there who buy on Amazon but would never even visit eBay. That makes it a different market, and it's more than just books.
- Google Base - Free listings, easy to upload in bulk, powered by Google, and no fees when using Google Checkout. That means that if you've got a product to sell, you need to list it on Google Base too.
- Other auction sites - Some smaller sites you might want to look at include uBid.com, WeBidz.com, Bid-Alot.com, ePier.com, OnlineAuction.com, Bidtopia.com, eBid.net, and Auction.com. Just do a Google search for "online auction sites" and read up on user reviews.

B. Multiple eBay IDs

Smart sellers know that an ID that's related to your product or category looks more professional. When new sellers have learned the ropes and decide that it's time to get serious, they'll often change their User IDs. This can be a great way to put a fresh new spin on the way your business is presented. eBay allows you to change your ID once every 30 days. You can create multiple IDs to match your different categories or product lines. Having unique user IDs lets you optimize each ID to effectively promote specific product and you can also cross-promote your own IDs within your listings.

Be careful there are some downsides to this strategy. You'll dilute your Feedback score and rating. If you have four accounts, you might collect a total of 20 Feedback points, but with only five per individual account. This can mean it will take you a lot longer to reach Feedback milestones with any of those accounts. If you re-register your old ID after 30 days, you can point to your new one from About Me. If you've built your business up to a reasonable level, there's no reason not to try it out. Some sellers create a separate ID for their buying, so they look like a more dedicated seller. This helps keep your buying activities more private, which might be handy if you're sourcing products on eBay.

Starting a second or third ID early can be useful if you start to sell on it later. The longer the ID has been active, the more credible it looks. Even if you set up several User IDs, don't be tempted to start shill bidding. That's when you or your friends bid on your listings to drive up the bid price. Do not under any circumstance bid on your own listings or encourage friends to shill bid for you. It's illegal and will get your eBay ID deleted. If you do decide to create multiple user ID's make sure the information you use does not overlap. eBay will connect the ID's and if one gets suspended then they will suspend the other too.

C. <u>More leads and sales</u>

When it comes to promoting your auctions to as wide an audience as possible, it pays to think creatively to find as many different outlets as you can.

a. Classified ad sites

Many classified ad sites are on the web, including Craigslist and Kijiji. There's no reason you can't use these sites to promote your auction listings. One classified ad on its own won't bring you a whole lot of traffic, but one ad on dozens of sites might. Creating an ad for each site is a lot of work. This is why you should consider using services that allow you to create one ad and distribute it to a number of ad and shopping sites such as Craigslist, Google Base, LiveDeal, Kijiji, and Vast. vFlyer is one service that allows you to create your own virtual flyers to advertise anything you want and distribute your ad to various ad sites and shopping sites like the ones above. It's free, but there is a catch, if people click the link to your ads, they'll see ads for relevant or possibly competing products. Test it to see if it works or drives your ads' visitors to other ads. Creating classified ads for your eBay auctions may seem like a strange idea, but, if you can get a few extra sales or potential customers out of it give it a try.

b. eBay Classified Ads

Do you sell a product or service that requires back-and-forth with a prospective buyer? If so, check out eBay Classified Ads. eBay Classified Ads aren't part of the regular auction process, so bids can't be placed on them. Sales made as a result of your listing have to take place outside eBay, which makes them less secure than regular auction listings. But they're a good way to provide information about your products or services to potential buyers. Classified Ads are designed for sellers who wouldn't use eBay's regular auction services to sell their wares. eBay doesn't want to take traffic and sales away from regular auction listings, Classified Ads are available only for listings in these categories -

- Websites and businesses for sale
- Trade show booths
- Real Estate
- Travel
- Specialty services
- "Everything else"

The "Everything else" category includes Memberships, Information Products, like eBooks, which can no longer be sold in regular auctions, Funeral and Cemetery Services, and Advertising Opportunities. It works like this - Use eBay's Sell Your Item form to create your ad, just as you would with a normal auction listing. Once you select one of the eligible categories, you can select Classified Ad as your selling format. You pay $9.95 for every 30 days. Provide your contact info and hours of operation, all of which will be displayed at the top of your listing. Classified Ads show up in regular search results under the same categories as regular listings. When buyers find a Classified Ad in the category they're searching, they then contact you through the phone number or email address you provide at the top of your listing.

Because transactions take place off eBay, there are no Final Value fees to pay. If you think about it, it's not that much to pay to get instant exposure to an audience as massive as eBay's. When customers contact you, you might be able to add them to your opt-in list. Take the opportunity to ask them if they'd like to sign up for your newsletter or receive information on related subjects in the future. eBay doesn't have any rules against this as long as you get their permission first. Consider putting an offer to join your newsletter in your response email.

D. <u>Buy It Now</u>

There is a large number of Buy It Now (BIN) auctions on eBay. In fact, fixed-price sales, mostly BIN, now account for the majority of the gross merchandise volume sold on eBay.

a. Use BIN in your auction listings

In an auction-style listing, you set a BIN price that gives potential buyers the opportunity to purchase your product right away, ending the auction early. The BIN option will disappear, however, as soon as someone bids on your item, turning it into a regular auction. There's always the chance that you'll get an impulse buyer who will purchase your item right away at the BIN price. The advantage to this strategy is that it costs less to list a product with a low insertion price and a high BIN price than it does to list your item with a high starting price.

b. Use BIN in a fixed-price item

A fixed-price BIN item is listed at a set price until it sells. This is great for selling time-sensitive items such as concert tickets or for holiday gifts where people are more willing to pay more to get something quickly. It's an excellent option if you have a steady supply of inventory or you sell popular items that are in high demand. The best way to maximize your profits selling fixed-price items is to turn over your stock more quickly. Buy It Now listings can end at any time, you can often sell three times as much product as you could within one seven-day auction listing. Don't be tempted to set your BIN price too high, your goal is to encourage fast sales for maximum profit. You can use fixed price listings for up to 30 days.

c. Potential disadvantages

For the most part, using the Buy It Now option is great for items that people might need right away. When your customer's car, cell phone, or microwave oven stops working, for instance, they need a new one now. Using Buy It Now might also limit how high the bidding can go, so if you're not careful, you may cheat yourself out of profits. Auctions with the BIN feature, including Store items, don't seem quite as urgent, so you may get fewer bids, which often means a lower selling price.

E. **Block risky bidders**

To avoid rip-offs, be sure to do a little research into your bidders, especially if you're selling a big-ticket item. A great place to start is by checking the Feedback they've received as a buyer. Simply click the Feedback number that linked next to their User ID and you'll see their Feedback page. There, you can click the Feedback as a buyer tab to see comments they've received from other sellers. Another option is for you to review their bidding history and look for suspicious patterns. Here's how to check bidder history -

- Click the Advanced Search link next to the search box on any page
- Click Items by Bidder in the box on the left
- Type the bidder's user ID in the box
- Click the Include completed listings checkbox and click Search

You can cancel a bid, but you must have a good reason to do so. Be prepared to explain your request to eBay, and bring evidence to back up any claims. You can block certain bidders from ever bidding on any of your listings by adding them to your Blocked Bidders list. That's a good option for getting rid of bidders who have given you headaches in the past, or whose history looks dicey. Your Blocked Bidders list applies to all of your listings. It might be best to set up buyer requirements. By selecting certain buyer requirements, you can manage the types of buyers you'll allow to bid on or buy your items. This will reduce the number of buyers who can make transactions difficult or more expensive, or with a history of unpaid items. You may want to eliminate bidders who -

- Are registered in countries where you don't ship
- Have received Unpaid Item strikes
- Don't have a PayPal account

Barring individuals or groups from your listings can keep out troublemakers but it'll also reduce the overall number of potential buyers you'll have for your items. Always think carefully before using these tools to limit access to your auctions.

F. Promotional flyers

As a business owner, you should always look for ways to promote your listings and increase your sales. But once you've actually sold an item, you have new opportunities to make money. One way to encourage one-time customers to become repeat customers is to put promotional flyers in the packages you ship to them. That way, you can drive your customers back to your eBay listings again and again. Not only are these flyers a fantastic way to thank your customers for their business and encourage positive feedback, they can also remind your customers to add you to their Favorite Sellers list. Once your customers list you as a Favorite Seller, eBay will automatically email them weekly updates of any new items you've got listed. Once your customers list you as a Favorite Seller, you'll get their email addresses, which means you can email them directly to build your relationship with them and send them more promotions whenever you want.

The more you're able to communicate with your customers, the better the chance they'll buy from you again and give you a five-star DSR score. Provided you've kept track of their buying history, you already know what kinds of items interest them, which means you have a good idea of what they might like to buy in the future. Presenting them with more opportunities to buy from you can potentially increase your sales while costing you nothing in return. The more ways you can find to encourage first-time buyers to become loyal, repeat customers, the better. To make the most of your customers, be sure to send them promotional flyers with these elements -

a. Thank-you

This lets your customer know you appreciate their business and shows them you are committed to meeting their needs.

b. Congratulations on purchasing this product

Many buyers report feeling a rush of excitement when they win an eBay auction but this excitement can dissipate by the time the item actually arrives in their hands. By congratulating your customer for snagging something of value, you can re-ignite the thrill of the win and get them interested in what else you've got to offer. It also helps to reduce buyer remorse, which can cut down on your refund rate if you accept returns.

c. A little about me

Putting a face to your business makes it more personal and can help create a connection with your customers. By including a short biography about you or your business, you can show your customers that there's a live person behind the listing.

d. If you liked this product, you may also be interested in

This is your chance to plug other items you have for sale which is effective when they're related to the item your customer originally bought. Be sure to include a brief description, your store address or the URL of the listing, and perhaps a small photo of the item. The key is to make your product blurb interesting enough that your customers will want to check it out online. This is also a good opportunity to remind your customers that they can get a weekly update of your items for sale automatically by adding you to their Favorite Sellers list.

e. Offer a discount on the buyer's next purchase

Offering a limited-time discount helps to create a sense of urgency to buy, if you compete with lots of other eBay sellers who sell the same kinds of items you do. It can really help your business stand out from the rest. On top of that, discounts are also a good way to liquidate slow-moving inventory, so you can replenish your stock with hot items that'll fly off the shelves.

f. Ask for 5-star Feedback

If you ask politely for a five-star rating, you're more likely to get it. Of course, the higher your DSR, the higher your listings will appear in eBay's search results.

Add a flyer to each package that tells your customers that you value their business and that you've done everything you can to ship their item quickly and cheaply. If you ask them to contact you with any concerns or complaints before they leave negative or neutral Feedback, they'll know you're committed to making them happy. Putting flyers in your shipping packages is an easy and inexpensive way to follow up with your customer and optimize the final step of the sales process. If you're an eBay Store owner, eBay has an easily-edited promotional flyer you can use in your shipments.

If you don't have a Store, or if you simply want more control of the look and layout of your flyer, go ahead and create one. Just be sure to customize it with your name, eBay Seller ID, and the URL of your website. It's also a good idea to keep your flyer to a maximum of one double-sided page in length. If it's any longer, you run the risk that it'll look like too much work to read and chances are it'll go straight into the recycling box.

G. Customer rewards

Occasionally eBay emails coupons to eBayers offering a discount for buying items with PayPal. These coupons contain a special code that the buyer enters during checkout to claim the discount. The most common coupon gives 10% off the final price of an item over $25. Most coupons can be used only by the email recipient, but some can be shared. Since eBay eats the discount, these shared coupons are another way for you to convert more of your listing browsers into buyers, and increase the final selling price of your items free. In your listing, mention that the winning bidder will be emailed a coupon code they can use to claim a special discount. This is a compelling incentive for your prospective customers to buy from you over your competitors and to place higher bids.

Search online for eBay coupon codes and you'll find a number of websites, blogs, and discussion groups that post shared coupon codes. Keep in mind that group coupon codes aren't available all the time, but they're worth hunting for, considering they might help you close sales. If you can find a site that sends out email alerts when the coupons are released, you'll save yourself a lot of time. Reward points can be another great motivator for people to place a bid. Through MyStoreRewards, Store sellers who accept PayPal can add a low-cost rewards program to their businesses to boost sales and profits. The program tracks buyer activity and calculates reward points, such as cash, and sends reports to the seller, automatically. MyStoreRewards requires no technical skills to set up, but there is a monthly fee calculated on the volume of sales.

H. Save on fees

You can earn a whopping 75% credit on your Final Value Fees when you send buyers to your eBay Store from a location outside eBay. It's called Store Referral Credit and it's another reason to expand your marketing efforts beyond eBay. Here are some of the ways you can drive traffic to your eBay Store -

- Put your Store URL into your email signature
- Encourage visitors to bookmark my store
- Post in the online forums
- Put your URL on your thank-you note
- Collect opt-in addresses and send out email promotions

To make sure eBay's system identifies your visitor as coming from a location, you'll need to add a unique code at the end of your URL. You can get more details on eBay's Store Referral Credit page.

I. Social media

a. Add value to listings with online video

eBay sellers can link videos within their listings. Here's how it works -

- Create a video using your digital camera or cell phone and save it to your computer.
- Upload your video to one of the following social sites, YouTube, Facebook, MySpace, or Microsoft Video.
- Tag your video with keywords that describe your item
- Link to your video in several places within your auction listing so people will see it.
- Display your Store or auction URL prominently within the video

Just make sure you own the rights or distribution rights to your video. You automatically own the rights to anything you create, as long as you only use things you create that means you can't use any music unless you have paid for the right to use it. You wouldn't want your video to get pulled over something as small as background tunes. eBay will not allow you to link to your video in your listing, you must embed it and the page displaying your video can't show products for sale off-eBay. For the people who find your listing through eBay, a link out to your video gives you a chance to -

- Demonstrate how your product works

- Show details about your item
- Build rapport with potential customers
- Build word of mouth on eBay
- Set your listing apart

And for the people who find your video while searching the video sites, it gives you a chance to -

- Increase the exposure of your listings
- Attract potential bidders from off eBay to your listing
- Attract potential buyers to your Store

People love online videos, so take advantage of the massive numbers of people searching on them and watch your traffic and sales spike. Your video will do best if it's useful or entertaining. eBay teamed up with several filmmakers to create sample video listings to spark some ideas. You should ensure that you're familiar with the most recent listing-links policy to ensure that you have put your video up on an eBay-legal site.

b. Publish auctions on Facebook

You can list your eBay auctions on your Facebook News Feed, which means all your Facebook friends will see your auctions when they appear giving you a much larger audience. First you'll need to open a Facebook account if you don't already have one. Go to your selling preferences in My eBay to link your Facebook profile to your eBay account or use the link on the Congratulations page after you've listed an item through the Sell Your Item form. Whenever you list a new item, it will automatically be published in your Facebook News Feed.

If you've never shared a listing with Facebook before, you'll get an invitation whenever you successfully list an item. Once you start sharing, all the items you list for sale on eBay will continue to be sent to Facebook, until you turn off sharing in My eBay. If you don't want to share, click Cancel on the confirmation page rather than Confirm. To stop or re-start sharing, you can go to My eBay and edit your sharing preferences whenever you want.

There are a couple of things you need to remember, though. eBay's shill bidding policy doesn't allow bids from anyone who has more access to your item information than the general eBay Community. This means your friends aren't allowed to bid on an auction-style listing. If you want your Facebook friends to be able to buy your items, you'll have to list them as Buy It Now or for a Fixed Price. It's still okay to offer auction-style bidding on your items but your Facebook friends won't be able to bid. eBay recommends that you block bids from their eBay accounts.

J. Want It Now

eBay's Want It Now service presents a golden opportunity to connect with thousands of buyers who are so desperate to purchase something, they're actually advertising for it. Here's how it works - Buyers post their Want It Now ads for free, and you can search their listings for keywords relating to items you have for sale. If you find a good match, you can respond by sending them a link to your auction. You don't even have to have your item already listed for sale to respond to a buyer. You can create a listing especially for them.

It's worth browsing the Want It Now listings in case you see an ad for something you happen to have lying around that you haven't got around to listing. You can also use Want It Now for market research. A quick browse through the Want It Now listings will help you assess the current demand. In the holiday, the Want It Now area of eBay is crammed with Christmas shoppers, wallets open and armed with the wish-lists of family and friends.

K. Sell with the seasons

How do you get more bids and more sales during the holiday buying frenzy, when every eBay seller is competing to take advantage of the flood of holiday buyers? You sweeten the deal, make your potential bidders offers they can't refuse, and you make those offers much more attractive than your competitors' offers.

a. Allow returns for a set period after the holidays

It's a good idea to offer a returns policy on all your items and during the busy holiday period. It can boost sales by removing that feeling of risk that nips so many sales in the bud. There's very little risk to you because if you state clearly that buyers must pay for return postage themselves, you will get very few returns.

b. Holiday discounts and coupons

One of the best things you can offer is a discount. Even the smallest saving can entice someone to bid on your item instead of a competitor's. There are several ways to do this -

- Reduce your prices
- Create your own PayPal discount codes, for an annual fee of $24.95, PayCodes lets you create multiple codes of your own.
- Find free PayPal coupons
- Offer deals on shipping

All of these incentives will boost your sales by making you stand out from the crowd, as long as you place them prominently on your listings so people know about them but before you select which ones you want to use, check out what your competitors are doing. That way, you'll know exactly what you need to do to make your offer stand out.

In Closing

Here they are, all the basic steps and techniques it takes to grow a successful eBay business. We hope you enjoyed this book and can use what we've shared to start and grow your business. If you did not write down the numerous links we shared with you throughout this book don't worry. Just visit the helpful links pdf provided on your bonus CD. Links are provided by the section they pertain to.

Please remember that eBay is always changing and some of the ideas, techniques, services, policies ect., in this book might have changed before we get a chance to update it. Also please bear in mind that this is not an in depth analysis of eBay and how to build a business. It is our belief that eBay should only be a stepping stone on your path to online business success.

With the constant change in eBay policies and rising fees it may be difficult to find lasting success on eBay but it is still a great place to begin because of the exposure you get to consumers. That is why we have included the basic steps you need. If you want a more advanced eBay education we suggest eBay for Dummies the All in One Desk Reference.

The techniques we have shared with you are ones we have used or use daily in our own business so if you are having trouble, have questions, or are interested in learning more about a particular technique.

Please contact us at - takteam@ourgrnbusiness.com.

Thank You!

Kristin and Tom